# Prayer Manual For Daily Intercession

## Effective Way To Pray And Intercede Like A Firebrand Intercessor

(Prayer Power Point Volume 2)

By Manasseh Omechamba

TRILOGY
PROFESSIONAL PUBLISHING MEETS POWERFUL PROMOTION
A wholly owned subsidiary of TBN

Prayer Manual for Daily Intercession

Trilogy Christian Publishers A Wholly Owned Subsidiary of Trinity Broadcasting Network

2442 Michelle Drive Tustin, CA 92780

Rights Department, 2442 Michelle Drive, Tustin, CA 92780.

Trilogy Christian Publishing/TBN and colophon are trademarks of Trinity Broadcasting Network.

Cover design by: Kristy Swank

For information about special discounts for bulk purchases, please contact Trilogy Christian Publishing.



Manufactured in the United States of America

10 9 8 7 6 5 4 3 2 1

Library of Congress Cataloging-in-Publication Data is available.

ISBN: 978-1-68556-911-2

E-ISBN: 978-1-68556-912-9

# Dedication

From my heart, this book is dedicated to my loving and caring parents, Elder K. Omechamba and Deaconess Mercy Omechamba, whom both have been greatly used by the Lord in the ministry of intercession at their local congregation (the Apostolic Church Mamfe-Cameroon) and for the body of Christ as a whole. No one has offered prayers for me than these great patriarchs of faith.

# Table of Contents

# FOREWORD

The most challenging time in the history of the church is now, when young people without Christ proudly preach messages of false hope and security. But amid all these, God has a few who have passion for Christ.

When I had an opportunity to closely observe Manasseh Omechamba in his final year in Bible school over a decade ago, I perceived something different. This present book, titled *Prayer Manual for Daily Intercession*, is most captivating and exceptionally clear, easy to read, understand, and claim God's unfailing promises.

This valuable text will serve many Christians who desire to pray right as a reliable prayer manual. Those who will derive advantage from this unique book can only be believers who are fully aware that God's promises constitute the unseen realities of the "evidence of things not seen," according to Hebrews 11:1 (KJB), which every Christian ought to hold fast until needs are met.

Manasseh simply wants to help you pray and intercede in a simple but right manner in line with scriptures. There is no better prayer manual than the one you are holding in your hands right now. This manual is intellectually stimulating, spiritually enhancing, and highly recommended.

—Dr. Dominic Enya Nsan

# Preface

There has always been this burning desire within me as to why the early church was so powerful that the supernatural was normal on a daily basis. I wanted to find out and implement the very practices that led to a supernatural lifestyle of the early church. I found out that *devotion* to these four things made the early church what it was: *teaching*, *fellowship*, *breaking of bread*, and *prayer*. In Acts 2:42 (NIV), it says, "They *devoted* themselves to the apostles' *teaching* and to *fellowship*, to the *breaking of bread* and to *prayer*."

Devotion to prayer and intercession was one aspect that our ministry needed in its early face and even today. One Thursday evening, during the last week of December 2021, while we were in church praying with my wife on behalf of our ministry, which just was now entering its seventh year by 2022, I heard vividly in my spirit to write a prayer manual for our intercessors so they can effectively pray for the needs of our ministry. By the next morning, I was able to sit for several hours putting down materials as I believed I was inspired by the Spirit of God to do so. To my amazement, fourteen pages were typed out on one seating. Right away, I knew God was at work in me and through me. By the first week of January 2022, prior to our twenty-one days of annual fasting and prayer, we had many prayer power points already available, and these were used by our team. By the end of the twenty-one days prayer-fast, we had close to a hundred scripturally back prayer points. Our leaders testified of how powerful those devotional prayer power points were. The Lord, then, impressed in my spirit to put together this piece of work not just for our ministry but that it be used by the global church. Our intercessors are now burning on fire just by using these materials. As you use this manual, be rest assured that your prayer life shall change dynamics.

# Introduction

Jesus' earthly ministry would never have been successful outside of prayer and intercession. The prayer life of Jesus should be a role model to every intercessor. Not only did He practice a personal private prayer lifestyle, but He also time and again took three of His disciples for intercession.

Mark 14:32–33 (NIV): "They went to a place called Gethsemane, and Jesus said to his disciples, 'Sit here while I pray.' He took Peter, James and John along with him, and he began to be deeply distressed and troubled." Peter, James, and John often accompanied Jesus for special prayer moments; they were His prayer partners and therefore formed the intercession team of Jesus' earthly ministry.

*About eight days after Jesus had said these things, He took with Him Peter, John, and James, and went up on a mountain to pray. And as He was praying, the appearance of His face changed, and His clothes became radiantly white. Suddenly two men, Moses and Elijah, began talking with Jesus. They appeared in glory and spoke about His departure, which He was about to accomplish at Jerusalem. Meanwhile Peter and his companions were overcome by sleep, but when they awoke, they saw Jesus' glory and the two men standing with Him.*

Luke 9:28–32 (BSB)

Luke 9:31 (NLT) says, "They were glorious to see."

Notice here that on the mountain of transfiguration, Jesus was again accompanied by Peter, James, and John for a special moment of prayer, and there appeared two other great intercessors by names Moses and Elijah. At the scene, Jesus was totally transformed into a spirit being, having a conversation with these two heavenly intercessors. The purpose of this prayer meeting on the mountain was to prepare Jesus through intercessory prayers prior to His arrest, suffering, death, and resurrection. The intercessory team was made up of six intercessors: Jesus, Moses, Elijah (who came from heaven), and Peter, James, and John (as earthly witnesses).

Another instance of Jesus with His three companions is when Jesus was going to Jairus' house to pray for the sick twelve-year-old girl who later had even passed on before Jesus arrived. Mark 5:37 (NIV) says, "He did not let anyone follow him except Peter, James and John the brother of James." And Luke 8:51 (NIV) says, "When he arrived at the house of Jairus, he did not let anyone go in with him except Peter, John and James, and the child's father and mother."

The Spirit of God in us gives us the ability to be intercessors. It brings about a supernatural transformation to enable us to do the things Jesus did. He is an intercessor, and so are we because we have His Spirit's DNA in our spirit.

Second Corinthians 3:18 says (NLT), "So all of us who have had that veil removed can see and reflect the glory of the Lord. And the Lord—who is the Spirit—makes us more and more like him as we are changed into his glorious image."

Without His Spirit, we will not effectively be used as intercessors. The Holy Spirit gives us credibility for effective intercession and a lifestyle of prayer.

Romans 8:26 (NLT): "And the Holy Spirit helps us in our weakness. For example, we don't know what God wants us to pray for. But the Holy Spirit prays for us with groanings that cannot be expressed in words."

A true intercessor is one that has overcome a selfish prayer lifestyle. This means they do not only pray for their needs but pray for others, and because of that, God blesses them.

Job 42:10 (AMP): "The LORD restored the fortunes of Job when he prayed for his friends, and the LORD gave Job twice as much as he had before."

This book was written to prepare and equip you for the ministry of intercession. You will learn how to use simple but powerful and effective Scriptures to pray according to the will of God. Your prayer dynamics are just about to shift. You are shifting from learning to pray to praying effectively. The devil is already feeling threatened by you going through this book. You are now a blessing to your family, your local church, your community, your city, your state, your nation, and nations of the earth and the global church of our Lord Jesus Christ.

Prayer for the Reader

In the name of the Lord Jesus, as you go through this book, may you catch the fire and passion for intercession. You will be used as the workmanship of God, prepared for every good work. By the grace of God, you are about to gain some heights and pounds in the spirit. You shall be a terror to the kingdom of darkness and a blessing to the kingdom of God. I wish you the best in your calling and ministry. You are a great asset to the church.

# Chapter One

## Section 1.1

## Never Pray Amiss Again

*For if I pray in a tongue, my spirit prays, but my mind is unfruitful. So what shall I do? I will pray with my spirit, but I will also pray with my understanding; I will sing with my spirit, but I will also sing with my understanding.*

1 Corinthians 14:14–15 (NIV)

James 4:3 (NASB): "You ask and do not receive, because you ask with the wrong motives, so that you may spend *what you request* on your pleasures."

Our prayers should be done with the right mindset, motives, and objectives. Therefore I carefully asked the Lord's heart to direct each prayer point in this manual.

This document is exclusively prepared for churches, ministries, believers, and those called into the intercession ministry. And even to lay believers seeking to learn how to pray in the will of God, this manual will be very beneficial. Every family needs a watchman, every church or ministry desperately needs intercessors, and everyone needs a prayer partner or at least someone praying for them. Please, from this day, start praying for your church, friends, community, nations, the lost, the poor, the helpless, the unsaved, and so forth.

## Section 1.2

# What Is "Intercession"?

Intercession is a spiritual mediation through prayer on behalf of a person or persons, group, or church. It is a spiritual intervention by someone for someone who needs assistance with prayer.

Whenever two or three persons gather in the name of the Lord, they can begin making intercession for a church.

Matthew 18:20 (NKJV): "For where two or three are gathered together in My name, I am there in the midst of them."

## Section 1.3

### Who Is an Intercessor?

An intercessor is a person who dedicates oneself to prayer and meditation on behalf of others. The act of intervening for others at the place of prayer is what intercessors do. Such persons stand in the presence of God as a spiritual mediator for others. Christ is our perfect example who stood in God's presence to reconcile the fallen man back to God.

First Timothy 2:5 (NKJV): "For *there is* one God and one Mediator between God and men, *the* Man Christ Jesus."

## SECTION 1.4

### How to Intercede

The one that intercedes or pleads for the case of others must be a "born-again believer" who has been saved, free from accusations, living a righteous life through the sanctifying blood of Jesus. One that is in right standing with God is qualified to intervene or intercede for people and the church. Intercession must be scripturally backed because the Word of God is powerful, giving life to death situations.

Hebrews 4:12 (NIV): "For the word of God is alive and active. Sharper than any double-edged sword, it penetrates even to dividing soul and spirit, joints and marrow; it judges the thoughts and attitudes of the heart."

The last part of John 6:63 (NKJV) says, "The words that I speak to you are spirit, and *they* are life."

The intercessor has to choose his words carefully, just as a defense attorney does when defending his client in the court of law.

# Section 1.5

## Benefits of the Intercessor and the Ministry of Intercession

1. The intercessor matures or grows spiritually through engaging in the Word, meditation, and prayer (Hebrews 5:14; Joshua 1:8).
2. Spiritual gifts are sharpened. But solid food belongs to those who are of full age, that is, those who *by reason of use* have their *senses exercised to discern* both good and evil (Hebrews 5:14).
3. As a watchman, they have heavenly rewards. After Job prayed for his friends, the Lord blessed him and restored him double (Job 42:10).
4. He is a terror to the kingdom of darkness and a blessing to the church.
5. They fulfill their calling in ministry. Men ought to pray and not faint (Luke 18:1).

6. The church will also benefit from this ministry as it watches over the body of Christ in the place of prayer. Mark 13:33 (NKJV) says, "Take heed, watch and pray; for you do not know when the time is."

7. That believer will be on fire for God. God does not like lukewarmness (Revelation 3:15–16).

# Section 2

## The Ministry of Intercession

The role of this ministry cannot be undermined. It is the life wire of the church. Jesus had intercessors during His earthly ministry. These were Peter, James, and John (His earthly witnesses) and Elijah and Moses (heavenly representatives).

Matthew 17:3 (NIV): "Just then there appeared before them Moses and Elijah, talking with Jesus." Our ministries and churches need the ministry of intercession as we see in the early church as recorded in the Book of Acts of the Apostles.

Prayers were constantly made for the church and the brethren. See, for instance, when the Apostles Peter and John were arrested and thrown in jail; then, we see the case of Paul and Silas. We are told that James was beheaded, but when the enemy came after Peter's life, the church embarked on serious prayers and intercession for Peter. If our local ministries or churches do well, the intercessors must engage in tireless prayer meetings. See the following passages from the Bible:

> *On their release, Peter and John went back to their own people and reported all that the chief priests and the elders had said to them. When they heard this, they raised their voices together in prayer to God. 'Sovereign Lord,' they said, 'you made the heavens and the earth and the sea, and everything in them.'*
>
> Acts 4:23–24 (NIV)

> *Now, Lord, consider their threats and enable your servants to speak your word with great boldness. Stretch out your hand to heal and perform signs and wonders through the name of your holy servant Jesus. After they prayed, the place where they were meeting was shaken. And they were all filled with the Holy Spirit and spoke the word of God boldly.*
>
> Acts 4:29–31 (NIV)

When we fail to pray, the enemy will attack and afflict God's people and even the church. You see, in the case of James being beheaded, no prayer was offered for him, but that was not the case with Peter.

> *It was about this time that King Herod arrested some who belonged to the church, intending to persecute them. He had James, the brother of John, put to death with the sword. When he saw that this met with approval among the Jews, he proceeded to seize Peter also. This happened during the Festival of Unleavened Bread. After arresting him, he put him in prison, handing him over to be guarded by four squads of four soldiers each. Herod intended to bring him out for public trial after the Passover. So Peter was kept in prison, but the church was earnestly praying to God for him.*
>
> Acts 12:1–5 (NIV)

The following verses tell of the result of intercession:

> *The night before Herod was to bring him to trial, Peter was sleeping between two soldiers, bound with two chains, and sentries stood guard at the entrance. Suddenly an angel of the Lord appeared, and a light shone in the cell. He struck Peter on the side and woke him up. 'Quick, get up!' he said, and the chains fell off Peter's wrists. Then the angel said to him, 'Put on your clothes and sandals.' And Peter did so. 'Wrap your cloak around you and follow me,' the angel told him, Peter followed him out of the prison, but he had no idea that what the angel was doing was really happening; he thought he was seeing a vision. They passed the first and second guards and came to the iron gate leading to the city. It opened for them by itself, and they went through it. When they had walked the length of one street, suddenly the angel left him. Then Peter came to himself and said, 'Now I know without a doubt that the Lord has sent his angel and rescued me from Herod's clutches and from everything the Jewish people were hoping would happen.' When this had dawned on him, he went to the house of Mary the mother of John, also called Mark, where many people had gathered and were praying.*
>
> Acts 12:6–12 (NIV)

Jesus told His followers to watch with Him through the night, but they were weak in the flesh, so He encouraged them to keep watch for at least an hour. See the following scriptures:

> *He took Peter, James and John along with him, and he began to be deeply distressed and troubled. 'My soul is overwhelmed with sorrow to the point of death,' he said to them. 'Stay here and keep watch.'*
>
> Mark 14:33–34 (NIV)

Here we see that Jesus perceived His suffering was near and asked for Peter, James, and John *to keep watch or intercede for Him.*

The ministry of intercession is about keeping watch, devoting oneself to prayer, to be on alert.

Ephesians 6:18 (BSB): "Pray in the Spirit at all times, with every kind of prayer and petition. To this end, stay alert with all perseverance in your prayers for all the saints."

Colossians 4:2 (NIV): "Devote yourselves to prayer, being watchful and thankful."

Mark 14:37 (NIV): "Then he returned to his disciples and found them sleeping. 'Simon,' he said to Peter, 'are you asleep? Couldn't you *keep watch* for one hour?'"

Luke 18:1 (KJB): "Men ought always to pray, and not to faint."

## Chapter Two

### Prayer Power Points

### Ready Prayer Bullets for Intercession

These prayer power points will help you catch the fire and the passion for intercession. You are not just praying, but you are building your spirit, and at the same time, you are charging up like dynamite, generating power from the inside.

1. Prayer for the gift of life:

John 10:10 (NIV): "The thief comes only to steal and kill and destroy; I have come that they may have life, and have it to the full."

*Pray after me:* Father, thank you for the gift of life. Satan, you will not steal my *joy*, neither will you destroy me, nor will you kill me before my time. Again, I give thanks to God for the fullness of life in Christ Jesus.

2. Prayer for deliverance and honor:

Psalm 91:15 (KJB): "He shall call upon Me, and I will answer him; I *will be* with him in trouble; I will deliver him and honor him."

*Pray like this:* Oh God of heaven and earth, deliver me from anything hunting my life, and remove me from the midst of trouble. I pray that You honor me with protection.

3. Prayer for the gift of salvation and long life:

Psalm 91:16 (KJB): "With long life I will satisfy him and show him my salvation."

*Repeat after me:* Father, thank you for the gift of salvation, and thank you for preservation, for immunity against any deadly disease; I thank you in advance for satisfying me with long life. May I see Your salvation all days of my life.

4. Prayer for the church against the gates of hell:

Matthew 16:18 (KJB, paraphrased): "And I say also unto thee, for you are Peter (which means rock), and upon this rock I will build my church; and the gates of hell shall not prevail against it."

*Pray after me:* Dear Lord, I thank you for keeping Your church, thank you for the team international church, and thank you for the shepherd of this church for overcoming the plot of Satan against this commission.

5. Prayer for crossing barriers and circumstances:

Luke 8:22 (NIV): "One day Jesus said to his disciples, 'Let us go over to the other side of the lake.' So, they got into a boat and set out."

*Pray with me:* Say, oh God, you are faithful in keeping Your promises, and You have brought our congregation, the church of our Lord Jesus Christ, this far; we are trusting that You shall take us across into a new season and beyond. Do not allow the storms of life to stop us. We declare our victory over all oppositions in Jesus' name.

6. Prayer of verdict against our enemies:

Exodus 15:4 (NASB): "Pharaoh's chariots and his army He has thrown into the sea; His chosen captains are drowned in the Red Sea."

*Say after me:* Father, we thank you for being a righteous judge. You have the final verdict, I know You will drown all the challenges we had in the past, and by Your grace, none shall crossover with us into our new seasons and years to come. May we not carry over the problems of the past but judge in our favor against the adversaries after our livelihood and well-being.

7. Prayer for turnaround blessing and breakthrough:

Romans 8:28 (NLT): "And we know that God causes everything to work together for the good of those who love God and are called according to his purpose for them."

*Pray after me:* Dear God of all possibilities, You called us according to Your purpose; You love us indeed. Father, may all that we have been through the past years as a ministry, Your church, turn around for our good in this new season and beyond.

8. Prayer for favor and double blessings:

Isaiah 61:7 (NLT): "Instead of shame and dishonor, you will enjoy a double share of honor. You will possess a double portion of prosperity in your land, and everlasting joy will be yours."

*Say after me:* In the name of Jesus, instead of shame, our church (call the name of your church) shall become famous for the kingdom; instead of dishonor, we shall receive a double honor; instead of trouble and problems, we shall travail and prevail. May our pain will produce promotions, and our mess turns into a miracle.

9. Prayer for possessing our possession:

Joshua 1:3 (NASB): "Every place on which the sole of your foot steps, I have given it to you, just as I spoke to Moses."

*Pray after me:* Oh God, by Your covenant promise, we possess this land where we are walking on; we take possession of this city. Thank you because Your promises are "Yes" and "Amen."

10. Prayer for lifting:

Job 22:29 (KJB): "When men are cast down, then thou shalt say, There is lifting up; and he shall save the humble person."

*Pray after me:* My Father, by Your grace, I am lifted above all circumstances and situations. Oh God, I will not settle for less because You are the lifter of men.

11. Prayer for upliftment:

Proverbs 24:16 (BSB): "For though a righteous man may fall seven times, he still gets up; but the wicked stumble in bad times."

*Pray with me:* Father, with Your right hand, may You lift me up from where I have fallen and set me on the path of righteousness.

12. Prayer for deliverance:

Psalm 34:19 (KJB): "Many are the afflictions of the righteous: but the LORD delivereth him out of them all."

*Pray after me:* Father, deliver me from all manner of afflictions; and safe me from evil and trouble days.

13. Prayer for deliverance against recurring afflictions:

Nahum 1:9 (BSB): "Whatever you plot against the LORD, He will bring to an end. Affliction will not rise up a second time."

*Pray after me:* Oh God, my Father, bring all the plot of the wicked against God's people to nothing. As I pray, I interrupt and intercept the hand of the enemy attempting to afflict God's children or me.

14. Prayer for a successful spiritual walk with God:

Joshua 1:8 (KJB): "This book of the law shall not depart out of thy mouth; but thou shalt meditate therein day and night, that thou mayest observe to do according to all that is written therein: for then thou shalt make thy way prosperous, and then thou shalt have good success."

*Pray after me:* My Lord my God, I ask for the grace to embrace the Word and to hold it in my hand and my heart. Increase my appetite for the Word.

15. Prayer for favor and understanding:

Proverbs 3:4 (KJB): "So shalt thou find favor and good understanding in the sight of God and man."

*Pray after me:* God of all grace, grant me favor and give me understanding of Your ways and the ways of men. Enlighten my heart and my head, so I may keep to Your precepts.

16. Prayer for favor in wisdom:

Luke 2:52 (ESV): "And Jesus increased in wisdom and stature and in favor with God and man."

*Pray with me:* Father God, I ask for special favor with You to increase in wisdom. May You also bless me so I may find favor among men. Let me also excel across different cultures.

17. Prayer for territory possession:

Deuteronomy 11:24 (KJB): "Every place where on the soles of your feet shall tread shall be yours."

*Pray after me:* (Prophetic action: You may choose to walk on bare feet as you pray.) I take possession of this territory where I am walking on, I possess my possessions, and by this prophetic act, I take this city for Jesus.

18. Prayer to subdue the wicked:

Malachi 4:3 (AMP): "'You will trample the wicked, for they will be ashes under the soles of your feet on the day that I do this,' says the LORD of hosts."

*Pray with me:* In the name of Jesus, I subdue the wicked under my feet, and I trample over them by day by night. My feet will not carry me to a place of my destruction.

19. Prayer for manifesting your identity in Christ:

Romans 8:19 (KJB): "For the earnest expectation of the creature waiteth for the manifestation of the sons of God."

*Pray after me:* Father, in the name of Jesus, I overcome whatever will want to stop me from fully manifesting all that God has called me to be in this life and the life to come.

20. Prayer for repentance:

First John 1:10 (KJB): "If we say that we have not sinned, we make him a liar, and his word is not in us."

*Repeat after me:* I confess all sins of omission and commission, I repent of my mistakes, and I also forgive anyone that offended me so that God will forgive me. I am a sinner saved by grace, not of works, and by the legal blood of Jesus, I was justified through faith. Jesus paid all my debts, past, present, and future; I am free.

21. Prayer for restoration:

Luke 15:18–19 (NIV): "I will set out and go back to my father and say to him: Father, I have sinned against heaven and against you. I am no longer worthy to be called your son; make me like one of your hired servants."

*Pray with me:* Father God, like the prodigal son, I return to You, have mercy on me. I am grateful for You accepting me. I chose to be Your slave, not even a son. Being a slave to You is better than being a slave to the devil. Lord, may You accept me just as I am. Thank you, Jesus.

22. Prayer for knowledge, wisdom, and understanding:

Colossians 1:9 (NLT): "So we have not stopped praying for you since we first heard about you. We ask God to give you complete knowledge of his will and to give you spiritual wisdom and understanding."

*Say after me:* Heavenly Father, give me this day an impartation through your Spirit; the knowledge, wisdom, and understanding of Your will for my life, assignment, family, ministry, career, and all that concerns me.

23. Prayer for establishment:

First Peter 5:10 (NKJV): "But may the God of all grace, who called us to His eternal glory by Christ Jesus, after you have suffered a while, perfect, establish, strengthen, and settle *you*."

*Pray with me:* Faithful Father, thank you for my trying season; I know it will not last. I pray Thee to look after my case; may You perfect all that concerns me, strengthen me, and establish my faith in You. By Your grace, settle me in all my deficits.

24. Prayer for bountiful grace (abundant, plentiful grace):

Second Corinthians 9:8 (NASB): "And God is able to make all grace overflow to you, so that, always having all sufficiency in everything, you may have an abundance for every good deed."

*Pray after me:* Oh God of all grace, release upon Your church (mention the name of your church) an overflowing grace this year, for good works, for ministry, for miracles, signs, and wonders, for teaching, preaching, soul-winning, charity, and all that pertains to the kingdom business.

25. Prayer against the wicked:

Psalm 68:1 (NASB): "For the music director. A Psalm of David. A Song. May God arise, may His enemies be scattered, and may those who hate Him flee from His presence."

*Pray with me:* In the name of Jesus, as I lift up my voice in prayer, Father God arise, disable and disperse the enemies of God's people; cause haters to flee from Your fearful consuming presence.

26. Prayer for supernatural supply:

Philippians 4:19 (NKJV): "And my God shall supply all your need according to His riches in glory by Christ Jesus."

*Pray with me:* My Lord, my God, by Your infinite grace, meet every need in all aspects of my life. Oh God of all grace, supplier of my every need, I thank you in advance for meeting the need of my family, my brethren, and the church as a whole.

27. Prayer to avert reproach:

Psalm 79:4 (ABPE): "We were a reproach to our neighbors, a mockery and a laughingstock to those around us."

*Pray after me:* In the name of Jesus, I refuse to be a laughingstock and a mockery in my generation. But rather let my ugly situations to a glorious breakthrough. May my life become a reference point and a testimony to the glory of God Almighty.

28. Prayer for endowment with grace and strength:

Isaiah 40:31 (NKJV): "But those who wait on the LORD shall renew *their* strength; they shall mount up with wings like eagles, they shall run and not be weary, they shall walk and not faint."

*Pray after me:* Father God, I ask for the grace to wait on You in the place of prayer and meditation on Your Word. Empower me like an eagle; instead of getting weary, may I receive supernatural strength, and may I not faint while serving You, Lord.

29. Prayer for grace to continue in service:

Galatians 6:9 (BSB): "Let us not grow weary in well-doing, for in due time we will reap a harvest if we do not give up."

*Say with me:* In the mighty name of Jesus, I reject the spirit of discouragement, I refuse to grow weary, I refuse to quit, and I refuse to give up before my crowning and harvest.

30. Prayer for grace to seek the Lord:

Hebrews 11:6 (KJB): "But without faith it is impossible to please Him, for he who comes to God must believe that He is, and that He is a rewarder of those who diligently seek Him."

*Pray with me:* Jehovah Jireh, my Provider and Rewarder, grant me the grace to seek You tirelessly and earnestly with all diligence. I am hungry and thirsty for Your righteousness. I receive Your grace now.

31. Prayer to remain in grace:

Romans 5:2 (KJB): "By whom also we have access by faith into this grace wherein we stand, and rejoice in hope of the glory of God."

*Repeat after me:* Heavenly Father, I pray Thee that I may not fall from grace, but rather obtain faith to access Your abiding grace and to hopefully enjoy Your blessing as You make that available for Your children.

32. Prayer against falling from grace:

First Corinthians 10:12 (NASB): "Therefore let the one who thinks he stands watch out that he does not fall."

*Pray with me:* Father God, teach me how to watch over my steps, and help me to stand and not fall from Your grace. May Your Holy Spirit guide me daily and convict me whenever I am going astray, so I may repent and be restored into the faith.

33. Prayer to avert disgrace:

Psalm 42:3 (BSB): "My tears have been my food both day and night, while men ask me all day long, 'Where is your God?'"

*Pray along with me:* My Father, my Fighter, do not allow my enemies to mock me, fight my battles, wipe my tears, and scatter their plans. I refuse defeat and let it not be said amongst the unbelievers, "Where is your God?"

34. Prayer for mercy and favor:

Psalm 30:5 (NKJV): "For His anger *is but for* a moment, His favor *is for* life; weeping may endure for a night, but joy *comes* in the morning."

*Pray with me:* Dear Lord Jesus, thank you for Your mercy. Your anger has not consumed me, but rather You have shown me everlasting favor, and I am excited to enter the dawn of a new day in my life, thank you for overflowing joy that money cannot buy.

35. Prayer for divine exchange:

Second Corinthians 8:9 (NKJV): "For you know the grace of our Lord Jesus Christ, that though He was rich, yet for your sakes He became poor, that you through His poverty might become rich."

*Pray after me:* Father God, thank you for Your Son, Jesus, who through the cross has crushed poverty for my sake. By the grace of our Lord Jesus Christ, released through the finished work on the cross, poverty is deleted from my lineage now and forevermore.

36. Prayer for the gift of grace:

Second Corinthians 13:14 (NASB): "The grace of the Lord Jesus Christ, and the love of God, and the fellowship of the Holy Spirit, be with all of you."

*Pray with me:* My Lord, my God. Your promises are ever true. Thank you for the gift of grace that was given through Jesus as an act of love and which is imparted to me by Your Holy Spirit.

37. Prayer for activating healing grace:

Isaiah 53:4–5 (NIV): "Surely he took up our pain and bore our suffering, yet we considered him punished by God, stricken by him, and afflicted. But he was pierced for our transgressions, he was crushed for our iniquities; the punishment that brought us peace was on him, and *by his wounds we are healed.*"

*Pray with me:* Dear Lord Jesus, I thank you for taking up my infirmities, pains, sorrows, and despair so that I may receive healing in my body. I believe by Your stripes, scourging, and bleeding wounds, I am healed by faith and grace through the cross. Cross any trace of sickness in my life this day, in Jesus' name.

38. Prayer for healing and restoration of health:

Psalm 147:3 (AMP): "He heals the brokenhearted and binds up their wounds [healing their pain and comforting their sorrow]."

*Pray after me:* My Father and my Healer, mend the broken pieces of my heart, bind up my wounds. Right now, I receive a spiritual first aid; apply Your *Balm of Gilead* upon me. I receive total healing and restoration to my spiritual and physical health today in Jesus' name.

39. Prayer for activating the grace of God:

Second Corinthians 9:8 (NKJV): "And God *is* able to make all grace abound toward you, that you, always having all sufficiency in all *things,* may have an abundance for every good work."

*Pray with me:* Dear Lord Jesus, You are the embodiment of grace and the full expression of God. You are a covenant-keeping God; I receive every promise of grace to do good works for the sake of God's kingdom business. Thank you for supplying His ever-increasing grace to us.

40. Prayer to activate the grace of giving:

Second Corinthians 8:7 (BSB): "But just as you excel in everything—in faith, in speech, in knowledge, in complete earnestness, and in the love we inspired in you—see that you also excel in this *grace of giving.*"

*Pray with me:* May the grace of our Lord Jesus that works in everything pertaining to godliness begin to excel in the area of giving so that I may also exercise love and giving in Christendom.

41. Prayer for excess of grace and faith:

First Timothy 1:14 (NKJV): "And the grace of our Lord was exceedingly abundant, with faith and love which are in Christ Jesus."

*Pray after me*: Father, as Your grace was working in the life of the apostles, may it also work for us this day, and may faith and love in Christ continue to increase in my life.

42. Prayer for great exploits:

Daniel 11:32 (NKJV): "But the people who know their God shall be strong, and carry out *great exploits*."

*Pray after me:* Father, in the name of Jesus, I pray and ask for great grace for great exploits. For every advantage and opportunity that come my way, I shall hold onto it by the grace of God.

43. Prayer for grace to live above sin and the works of the devil:

First John 3:8 (NASB, paraphrased): "The one who practices sin is of the devil; for the devil has been sinning from the beginning. For this purpose, the Son of God was manifested, that He might destroy the works of the devil."

*Pray after me*: Dear Lord, Son of David, have mercy on me; I denounce sin, Satan, and the world. The works of the devil shall not manifest in me because you destroyed them on the cross.

44. Prayer for grace by measure:

Ephesians 4:7 (ASV): "But unto each one of us was the grace given according to the measure of the gift of Christ."

*Pray like this*: Dear Lord Jesus, I receive by faith any level of grace You are willing to measure for me this day, tomorrow, and forevermore, enlarge my capacity to receive more grace daily.

45. Prayer for endless supply of grace:

Ephesians 3:8 (NKJV): "To me, who am less than the least of all the saints, this grace was given, that I should preach among the Gentiles the unsearchable riches of Christ."

*Pray with me*: Father, in the name of Jesus, as You blessed Paul with so much grace without merit, I ask that I too be partaker of Your ever-supplying grace. I believe You have not changed, and You can do the same today like You did before on natural people who became supernatural.

46. Prayer for spiritual appetite:

Matthew 5:6 (NIV): "Blessed are those who hunger and thirst for righteousness, for they will be filled."

*Pray with me:* My Lord, my God. As the deer pants for water, so my soul longs after You, keep hungry for more, I desire Your righteousness and fill me now with Your Spirit and grace; I am desperate for You, Lord Jesus.

47. Prayer for multiplied peace and grace:

Second Peter 1:2 (KJB): "Grace and peace be multiplied unto you through the knowledge of God, and of Jesus our Lord."

The more Jesus you have, the more grace you have!

*Pray after me:* Father, I ask for more of You, more of Your love, more of the mind of Christ, more of Your nature and character, and may You multiply your grace in Your church, in my life and ministry.

48. Prayer for measure of faith and humility:

Romans 12:3 (NASB): "For through the grace given to me I say to everyone among you not to think more highly of himself than he ought to think; but to think so as to have sound judgment, as God has allotted to each a measure of faith."

*Pray after me:* Father God, please teach me how to stay humble. I give no room to pride, and I am open to any measure of faith You want to give me today. Thank you for being my source of faith.

49. Prayer against scorners and mockers:

Proverbs 3:34 (NKJV): "Surely He scorns the scornful, but gives grace to the humble."

*Say after me:* Father by Your power and lordship, mock our mockers, scorn our scorners, scoff the scoffers, and for our sake, resist and humble the proud.

50. Prayer for more of God's grace:

James 4:6 (NKJV): "But He gives more grace. Therefore, He says: 'God resists the proud, but gives grace to the humble.'"

*Pray after this manner:* Dear Lord Jesus, in Your name, I pray that You humble my heart, I ask for more of God's grace, and I humble to receive all that has been released for me this year and beyond.

51. Prayer for humility:

First Peter 5:5 (NASB): "You younger men, likewise, be subject to *your* elders; and all of you, clothe yourselves with humility toward one another because GOD IS OPPOSED TO THE PROUD, BUT HE GIVES GRACE TO THE HUMBLE."

*Pray with me:* Oh God, teach me humility and show me Your ways, endow me with grace for humility to leadership and those You have set in authority over me. Take away every bit of pride in me; give me a humble heart in Jesus' name.

52. Prayer for provision and preservation:

Exodus 23:25 (NKJV): "So you shall serve the LORD your God, and He will bless your bread and your water. And I will take sickness away from the midst of you."

*Pray after me:* Jehovah Jireh, You are my Provider, Jehovah Rapha, You are my Healer, I thank you for blessing me this day with divine health, and I thank you for taking away sickness and diseases amongst Your covenanted people.

53. Prayer for divine healing and health:

Exodus 15:26 (NASB): "And He said, 'If you will listen carefully to the voice of the LORD your God, and do what is right in His sight, and listen to His commandments, and keep all His statutes, I will put none of the diseases on you which I have put on the Egyptians; for I, the LORD, am your healer.'"

*Pray after this manner:* Father God, I know You love me, and You want the best for me. Teach me how to keep Your precepts, protect me from diseases and pestilences that may want to afflict me and my household, and by Your covenant promise, I am exempted from infirmities of the land.

54. Prayer to overcome discouragement:

Second Corinthians 4:8–9 (NKJV): "*We are* hard-pressed on every side, yet not crushed; *we are* perplexed, but not in despair; persecuted, but not forsaken; struck down, but not destroyed."

*Pray after this manner:* Dear Lord Jesus, send Your angels, Your ministering being, to assist me on challenging days; let Your Holy Spirit, the comforter, be my helper in times of despair; I ask in Jesus' name.

55. Prayer for reassurance:

Galatians 6:17 (NKJV): "From now on let no one trouble me, for I bear in my body the marks of the Lord Jesus."

*Pray after me:* In the name of our Lord Jesus, I believe and confess that I have the DNA of Christ in me. I bear His supernatural genetic material in me; I am of Christ who has justified me by His blood. Therefore, Satan, back off, for you have no claims on me.

56. Prayer for sharing with Christ's suffering:

Second Corinthians 4:10 (NLT): "Through suffering, our bodies continue to share in the death of Jesus so that the life of Jesus may also be seen in our bodies."

*Pray after me:* By the grace of God, I offer my body as a living sacrifice unto God and to be a vessel for the Holy Spirit's dwelling, now ready for the Master's use. Father, give me the strength to take up my cross and follow Jesus.

57. Prayer for mind reset:

First Peter 4:13 (BSB): "But rejoice that you share in the sufferings of Christ, so that you may be overjoyed at the revelation of His glory."

*Pray with me:* Oh God of all grace, reset my mind, and strengthen my heart that I may see beyond my today's suffering for Christ's sake, for the joy of the Lord is my strength, and there is much hope for what the future holds, I know that I will be overjoyed when Your glory is finally revealed.

58. Prayer to stay focused while suffering for the kingdom:

Romans 8:18 (NKJV): "For I consider that the sufferings of this present time are not worthy *to be compared* with the glory which shall be revealed in us."

*Pray after me:* Jehovah, my Redeemer and my Rewarder, I know my labor for the kingdom shall never be in vain. I have this hope in me that the coming glory shall override my present suffering; Christ in me is the hope of glory, and the joy of the Lord is my strength.

59. Prayer for God's guidance:

Proverbs 5:21 (NIV): "For your ways are in full view of the LORD, and he examines all your paths."

*Pray with me:* Lord, you know me more than I know myself; You understand the contents of my heart and motives; You know all my desires. Your ways are far better than my ways. Help me to stay on the paths of righteousness.

60. Prayer to align with God's thought patterns:

Isaiah 55:8–9 (NKJV): "'For My thoughts *are* not your thoughts, nor *are* your ways My ways,' says the LORD. 'For *as* the heavens are higher than the earth, so are My ways higher than your ways, and My thoughts than your thoughts.'"

*Pray after this manner:* Father, teach me Your ways and cause me to align with Your thoughts, Your will, and Your purpose, for my ways and thoughts are meaningless without Your leading. Help me, Lord.

61. Prayer to seek the ways of God:

Psalm 103:7 (NKJV): "He made known His ways to Moses, His acts to the children of Israel."

*Pray after me:* Almighty God, I pray that You reveal Your ways to me as You are willing; I refused to be carried by Your deeds or anything that mimics Your acts; I want to know You more.

62. Prayer for God's will to always prevail:

Isaiah 55:10–11 (NKJV): "For as the rain comes down, and the snow from heaven, and do not return there, but water the earth, and make it bring forth and bud, that it may give seed to the sower and bread to the eater, so shall My word be that goes forth from My mouth; *It shall not return to Me void*, but it shall accomplish what I please, and it shall prosper *in the thing* for which I sent it."

*Pray with me:* Father God, Your Word is powerful and will never fail. I pray that Your Word avails in all seasons of my life. Bring to pass every blessing that proceeds out of Your mouth as it pleases You. Your Word is living and effective to always produce tangible results.

63. Prayer for a renewed heart and a transformed mind:

Psalm 51:10–12 (NASB): "Create in me a clean heart, Oh God; and renew a right spirit within me. Cast me not away from thy presence; and take not thy Holy Spirit from me. Restore to me the joy of Your salvation and sustain me with a willing spirit."

*Pray after this manner:* Heavenly Father, I ask for a clean heart and a right spirit so that I may find favor in Your presence. Give me a heart that will accommodate Your Spirit within me and maintain my salvation. Dear Lord, restore me fully.

64. Prayer for mercy and grace:

Exodus 34:9 (NKJV): "Then he said, 'If now I have found grace in Your sight, O Lord, let my Lord, I pray, go among us, even though we *are* a stiff-necked people; and pardon our iniquity and our sin, and take us as Your inheritance.'"

*Pray with me:* Oh Lord, my God, have mercy on me (us) and show me favor. I am the work of Your hand, do not forsake me, but pardon my mistakes. Let me find grace in Your side this day.

65. Prayer for forgiveness:

Numbers 14:19 (BSB): "Pardon, I pray, the iniquity of this people, in keeping with the greatness of Your loving devotion, just as You have forgiven them ever since they left Egypt."

*Repeat after me:* Heavenly Father, I ask for forgiveness for my shortcomings. You have always shown me mercy. Thank you for answering my prayers in Jesus' name.

66. Prayer for total yielding to God:

John 3:30 (KJB): "He must increase, but I *must* decrease."

*Pray after me:* Father God, I choose to die to self, I die to the flesh,

I die to my will, I empty myself at the cross. May your will supersede my will, and You let Your purpose override my plans. I surrender my all to You. Amen and amen.

67. Prayer to release a new wave of glory:

Haggai 2:9 (NIV): "'The glory of this present house will be greater than the glory of the former house,' says the LORD Almighty. 'And in this place, I will grant peace,' declares the LORD Almighty."

*Pray after this manner:* God who created heaven and earth, we thank You for yesterday's glory, and we thank you more for today's glory. We thank you for the former and latter glory, and by Your grace, it will only get better and better as we go from glory to glory. Amen and amen.

68. Prayer to release the wealth stored up in glory:

Haggai 2:6–8 (NIV): "This is what the LORD Almighty says: 'In a little while I will once more shake the heavens and the earth, the sea and the dry land. I will shake all nations, and what is desired by all nations will come, and I will fill this house with glory,' says the LORD Almighty. 'The silver is mine and the gold is mine,' declares the LORD Almighty."

*Pray with me:* Almighty God, may Your shakings produce desirable results for the church, the body of Christ, and Your chosen people and nation. Fill us with Your glory this day that we experience a drastic, dramatic shift in wealth. May Your shakings result in supernatural wealth transfer to Your chosen people.

69. Prayer for supernatural deliverance from oppression:

Daniel 3:17–18 (NIV): "If we are thrown into the blazing furnace, the God we serve is able to deliver us from it, and he will deliver us from Your Majesty's hand. But even if he does not, we want you to know, Your Majesty, that we will not serve your gods or worship the image of gold you have set up."

*Pray with me:* Yeshua Hamashiach, I pray Thee to deliver me from all forms of demonic oppression; Jesus, the Messiah, save me from diabolic forces of oppression in dreams and real life

70. Prayer for supernatural immunity against strange fire:

Daniel 3:22 (NIV): "The king's command was so urgent and the furnace so hot that the flames of the fire killed the soldiers who took up Shadrach, Meshach and Abednego."

*Pray after me:* Any strange fire set up by our adversaries shall turn against them and shall surely consume them to ashes. Oh Lord, my Father, fight for me and deliver me from trouble.

71. Prayer for supernatural assistance on divine help:

Daniel 3:25–26 (NKJV): "'Look!' he answered, 'I see four men loose, walking in the midst of the fire: and they are not hurt, and the form of the fourth is like the Son of God.' Then Nebuchadnezzar went near the mouth of the burning fiery furnace *and* spoke, saying, 'Shadrach, Meshach, and Abed-Nego, servants of the Most High God, come out, and come *here*.' Then Shadrach, Meshach, and Abed-Nego came from the midst of the fire.

*Pray after me:* Lord God, my Savior, by Your power and protection over me, I shall come out from every satanic problem, persecution, and affliction from the demonic kingdom that comes my way; I shall walk out of it supernaturally with no hurt. Father, amaze my enemies by Your saving grace working in my life today and forevermore.

72. Prayer for favor and promotion:

Daniel 3:30 (NIV): "Then the king promoted Shadrach, Meshach and Abednego in the province of Babylon."

*Pray after me:* Jehovah Nissi (the Lord, my refuge), Elohim Shomri (God is my Protector), may the problems caused by my enemies set me up for a promotion. Give me such favor like You did for Joseph, Shadrach, Meshach, and Abednego.

73. Prayer for supernatural immunity against satanic circumstances:

Isaiah 43:2 (NIV): "When you pass through the waters, I will be with you; and when you pass through the rivers, they will not sweep over you. When you walk through the fire, you will not be burned; the flames will not set you ablaze."

*Pray with me:* Jesus, my Deliverer, may You not allow any evil circumstances to devour me. Uphold me when I go through a valley experience, do not allow rivers of problems to drown me, and protect me from being consumed by any form of strange fire.

74. Prayer against satanic destructive devices:

Isaiah 59:19 (NKJV): "So shall they fear the name of the LORD from the west, and His glory from the rising of the sun, when the enemy comes in like a flood, the Spirit of the LORD will lift up a standard against him."

*Pray after me:* Spirit of the Living God, may You lift a standard for me against any satanic attacks. Confiscate all satanic gadgets used in monitoring me. Deviate all fiery darts of the enemy, fired against me, and lift me up above all traps of the wicked.

75. Prayer for upliftment:

Psalm 75:6–7 (KJB): "For promotion cometh neither from the east, nor from the west, nor from the south. But God is the judge: he putteth down one, and setteth up another."

*Pray with me:* Unquestionable God, You have the power to appoint or dismiss; you can *hire, fire* and *re-hire*, yet no one can question You; Father, may You bring me to the level You have prepared for me; I will testify and give You all glory. Thanks for remembering my family and me in Jesus' name.

76. Prayer for renewed strength:

Philippians 4:13 (NKJV): "I can do all things through Christ who strengthens me."

*Pray after me:* Father God, by Your grace working in me, I shall carry out and complete every kingdom assignment given to me. I will do all that God says I will do; I shall soar from strength to strength.

77. Prayer for increasing knowledge:

Habakkuk 2:14 (NIV): "For the earth will be filled with the knowledge of the glory of the LORD as the waters cover the sea."

*Pray after me:* Almighty God, Maker of heaven and earth. May we increase our knowledge of the Word. Let the knowledge of our Lord Jesus spread and fill the earth. In these last days, pour out Your glory upon the earth in greater measures. This we ask in the name of Jesus, the Son of the Living God.

78. Prayer for increasing glory:

Isaiah 40:5 (NKJV): "The glory of the LORD shall be revealed, and all flesh shall see *it* together; for the mouth of the LORD has spoken."

*Pray after me:* Oh Lord of hosts, reveal Your glory as you have promised, and let everyone see and know that you are the Lord and have not changed. O Lord, reveal Your glory to the church, the body of Christ, and in your Holy Sanctuary of the assembly of the brethren.

79. Prayer for supernatural multiplicity and endless food supply:

Luke 9:16–17 (NIV): "Taking the five loaves and the two fish and looking up to heaven, he gave thanks and broke them. Then he gave them to the disciples to distribute to the people. They all ate and were satisfied, and the disciples picked up twelve basketfuls of broken pieces that were left over."

*Pray with me:* Faithful and Mighty God, You are our source; we know that You are able to fully satisfy our needs and can always supply to meet all our demands. Thank you for bountiful and overflowing food and drinks that we may never lack anything. We are blessed to be a blessing.

80. Prayer for our needs to be met:

Philippians 4:19 (NIV): "And my God will meet all your needs according to the riches of his glory in Christ Jesus."

*Pray after me:* Dear Lord of heaven, Your riches are enveloped in Your glory. Father, bring me to that place where I shall see no lack; I want to enjoy Your glory, show me Your glory, I ask in Jesus' name.

81. Prayer for God's favor and leading:

Exodus 33:13 (NKJV): "Now therefore, I pray, if I have found grace in Your sight, show me now Your way, that I may know You and that I may find grace in Your sight. And consider that this nation *is* Your people."

*Pray after me:* Loving Father, I ask with a humble heart that You show me Your way, and grant me favor on Your side and lead me day by day, and as a people after Your heart direct our path; this we pray in Jesus' mighty name.

82. Prayer for divine acceleration and speed:

John 6:19–21 (NKJV): "So when they had rowed about three or four miles, they saw Jesus walking on the sea and drawing near the boat; and they were afraid. But He said to them, 'It is I; do not be afraid.' *Then they willingly received Him into the boat, and immediately the boat was at the land where they were going."*

*Pray with me:* God of all possibilities, grant us (the church, the body of Christ) access to the supernatural; we believe that the days of Your power in signs and wonders are not over yet. Today I make a commitment to welcome You in all I do; grant me acceleration and speed.

83. Prayer for God's leading:

Proverbs 3:5–6 (NKJV): "Trust in the LORD with all your heart, and lean not on your own understanding; in all your ways acknowledge Him, and He shall direct your paths."

*Pray after me:* Jehovah, my Director, I will always put my trust in You, but will not put my confidence in man. I would rather make my boasts on God; I acknowledge that Your leading is beyond my reasoning, so help me, God.

84. Prayer to detour from demonic setups:

Psalm 91:3 (NASB): "For it is He who rescues you from the net of the trapper and from the deadly plague."

*Pray with me:* Oh God, my Defender, may You rescue me from any diabolic traps and deadly pestilences or killer diseases.

85. Prayer for long life and honor:

Psalm 91:15–16 (NKJV): "He shall call upon Me, and I will answer him; I *will be* with him in trouble; I will deliver him and honor him. With long life I will satisfy him, and show him My salvation."

*Pray with me:* My Father, You are the Giver of life and the Lifter of men. I ask in the name of the Lord to deliver me from all manner of troubles; I pray that You will satisfy me with long life and honor. I will live a long, honorable life. I reject a long, miserable life. Amen.

86. Prayer for preparation to meet opportunity:

Ecclesiastes 9:11 (NKJV): "I returned and saw under the sun that—the race *is* not to the swift, nor the battle to the strong, nor bread to the wise, nor riches to men of understanding, nor favor to men of skill; but time and chance happen to them all."

*Pray after me:* By your grace, my strength is renewed daily; I will not grow weary in the race I run and the battles I face, for I know that You are a generous God, giving wisdom, understanding, and favor as it pleases You. Dear Lord, help me locate and embrace the opportunities that come my way daily, in Jesus' name.

87. Prayer for soul-winning:

Proverbs 11:30 (NKJV): "The fruit of the righteous *is a* tree of life, and he who wins souls *is* wise."

*Pray after me:* Righteous Father, teach me wisdom. Bring me across a soul that must be won today; use me to save a soul this day. Amen.

88. Prayer that will save a soul:

James 5:20 (BSB): "Consider this: Whoever turns a sinner from the error of his way will save his soul from death and cover over a multitude of sins."

*Pray after me:* My God, give me what it takes to deliver a soul today; use me to rescue someone living in error so that soul shall be delivered from sin and death.

89. Prayer for guidance and direction:

Psalm 37:23–24 (NKJV): "The steps of a *good* man are ordered by the LORD, and He delights in his way. Though he fall, he shall not be utterly cast down; for the LORD upholds *him with* His hand."

*Pray with me:* Dear Lord Jesus, my strength comes from You, may Your Spirit guide me daily, though I make mistakes sometimes, may I not be totally cast down, but rather may You pick me up again and set me on the right path. Redeem me from the path of destruction in Jesus' name.

90. Prayer for anointing to get wealth:

Deuteronomy 8:17–18 (NASB): "Otherwise, you may say in your heart, 'My power and the strength of my hand made me this wealth.' But you are to remember the LORD your God, for it is He who is giving you power to make wealth, in order to confirm His covenant which He swore to your fathers, as *it is* this day."

*Pray with me:* Father God, You are my source, all I have and will ever have streams from You. What I am and will ever be is not by might, not by power, but by Your grace. You have anointed my hands to make wealth; I will always remember and praise You.

91. Prayer for cleansing the heart:

Psalm 66:18 (KJB): "If I regard iniquity in my heart, the Lord will not hear me."

*Pray with me:* Father, take away my sins, cause me not to be sin conscious and self-condemnation. I receive Your love and forgiveness through Your blood. Pardon me for all my mistakes and wrongdoings.

92. Prayer for godly direction:

Proverbs 14:12 (NKJV): "There is a way *that seems* right to a man, but its end *is* the way of death."

*Pray after me:* Oh Lord, my God, may I not be deceived by my selfish and biased ways, but lead me in the path of righteousness for Your name's sake so that I will not misrepresent You anywhere anytime, in Jesus' name. Amen.

93. Prayer for godly counsel:

Proverbs 12:15 (BSB): "The way of a fool is right in his own eyes, but a wise man listens to counsel."

*Pray after this manner:* Father, in the name of our Lord and Savior, Jesus Christ, I receive Your wisdom and counsel through the written Word of God; take away blindness and deceit from my heart and my head. I ask for revelation of Your Word. I reject foolishness and embrace godly counsel as often as it is made available to me. Amen.

94. Prayer to remove hindrances from receiving deliverance:

Isaiah 59:1–2 (NASB): "Behold, the LORD'S hand is not so short that it cannot save; nor is His ear so dull that it cannot hear. But your wrongdoings have caused a separation between you and your God, and your sins have hidden *His* face from you so that He does not hear."

*Pray with me:* Merciful God, today I repent from my wrongdoings and ways. May You not hide Your face from me, Lord, or close Your ears from my petitions, but in humility, I ask that You deliver me from my flaws, weaknesses, and shortcomings. In Jesus' name.

95. Prayer to ask God for forgiveness:

Isaiah 1:15 (BSB): "When you spread out your hands in prayer, I will hide My eyes from you; even though you multiply your prayers, I will not listen. Your hands are covered with blood."

*Pray after me:* Merciful God, blot my iniquity and transgressions. May You not close Your eyes from me. Cleanse me with Your blood, and I will be clean. May Your blood speak over my bloody and wicked ways that I may find mercy and forgiveness from You.

96. Prayer to turn from wicked ways:

Second Chronicles 7:14 (NKJV): "If My people who are called by My name will humble themselves, and pray and seek My face, and turn from their wicked ways, then I will hear from heaven, and will forgive their sin and heal their land."

*Pray after this manner:* Dear Lord God, we come to You in humility, seeking Your face and asking for forgiveness. We repent from our wicked ways. Father, may You hear us, forgive us, heal us and restore peace and order in our land.

97. Prayer for opening heaven over your church:

Second Chronicles 7:15 (NKJV): "Now My eyes will be open and My ears attentive to prayer *made* in this place."

*Pray with me:* Father God, according to Your Word, focus Your attention on our house of prayer. May heaven open over us today for a supernatural encounter and visitations. Increase angelic activities here now and whenever we gather in Your name.

98. Prayer inviting God's attention:

Second Chronicles 6:40 (BSB): "Now, my God, may Your eyes be open and Your ears attentive to the prayer offered in this place."

*Pray with me:* Dear Lord Jesus, incline Your ears and eyes to my prayers. In this place, may Your presence manifest and Your glory be revealed. Hear the cry of Your covenant people.

99. Prayer for God to fulfill His promises:

Numbers 23:19 (NKJV): "God *is* not a man, that He should lie, nor a s on of man, that He should repent. Has He said, and will He not do? Or has He spoken, and will He not make it good?"

*Pray after me:* Heavenly Father, Your promises stand sure, and they are yes and amen; what You say is what You do; You honor Your Word more than Your name. I pray that be the performance and fulfillment of those things You have said concerning me.

100. Prayer against evil omens:

Numbers 23:23 (KJB): "Surely there is no enchantment against Jacob, neither is there any divination against Israel: according to this time it shall be said of Jacob and of Israel, What hath God wrought!"

*Pray with me:* By the authority in the name above everything with a name, the covenanted and anointed name of Jesus, full of authority, I pray this day that no evil pronouncement against me and my household shall stand. Hired enchanters and diviners against me will be disappointed, and my life shall be full of testimonies.

101. Prayer to exercise authority and power in situations:

Matthew 16:19 (NKJV): "And I will give you the keys of the kingdom of heaven, and whatever you bind on earth will be bound in heaven, and whatever you loose on earth will be loosed in heaven."

Matthew 18:18 (NKJV): "Truly I say to you, whatever you bind on earth shall have been bound in heaven; and whatever you loose on earth shall have been loosed in heaven."

*Pray with me:* a) In the name of Jesus, by the power of attorney given to me, and by the legal blood of Jesus, I bind the forces of darkness at work in the situations at hand, in my life, in my family, in my place of work and in my area of assignment or ministry; you agent of Satan, the strongman, I conjure you to come out and never to return, in Jesus' name.

b) By the legal rights vested on me, in the name of Jesus, I release angels, ministering spirits, and the hosts of heaven; I deploy them to my area of challenge to assist me in bringing down the will and the kingdom of God on earth as it is in heaven. Let them break the chains of Satan around the people here present.

102. Prayer for divine endorsement:

Acts 2:22 (NASB): "Men of Israel, listen to these words: Jesus the Nazarene, a Man attested to you by God with miracles and wonders and signs which God performed through Him in your midst, just as you yourselves know."

*Pray after me:* My Father, in the name of Jesus, put a stamp of approval on me, release grace on my ears, eyes, mouth, and hands to hear, to see, to say, and to do what You have authorized and sent me for. I count on You, Lord, for divine approval and not man's approval.

103. Prayer to ask for anointing to do good works:

Acts 10:38 (NKJV): "How God anointed Jesus of Nazareth with the Holy Spirit and with power, who went about doing good and healing all who were oppressed by the devil, for God was with Him."

*Pray with me:* Oh God of all grace, I pray right now, as You anointed Jesus, a man from Nazareth, anoint me that I will be able to step out and do good as the occasion arises. Anoint my voice for teaching, preaching, and prophecy; anoint my hands for miracles, signs, and wonders. I know You are with me.

104. Prayer for greater grace for greater works:

John 14:12 (NASB): "Truly, truly I say to you, the one who believes in Me, the works that I do, he will do also; and greater *works* than these he will do, because I am going to the Father."

*Pray with me:* Heavenly Father, I believe that Jesus came in the flesh and walked the streets of Galilee doing the work of the kingdom. The Word says, if I believe, I will do the things Jesus did. I pray that you impart on me greater grace for greater works. Oh God, I am hungry for Your grace; I believe and receive it now.

105. Prayer demanding God's grace and anointing:

Acts 5:12 (NLT): "The apostles were performing many miraculous signs and wonders among the people. And all the believers were meeting regularly at the Temple in the area known as Solomon's Colonnade."

*Pray after me:* Jesus, the same, yesterday, today, and forever, just as You empowered Your followers for miracles, signs, and wonders as recorded in the Book of Acts of the Apostles; I know You are still doing the same today. Today, I make a demand on Your anointing and grace. Remember, I am Your follower too; bless me now in Jesus' name.

106. Prayer to believe and receive keys of the kingdom:

Matthew 16:19 (NKJV): "And I will give you the keys of the kingdom of heaven, and whatever you bind on earth will be bound in heaven, and whatever you loose on earth will be loosed in heaven."

*Pray after this manner:* Jesus, You promised that You would give Your disciples the keys of the kingdom. Father, I have decided to follow You and partake in everything related to Your kingdom mandate. I ask that You give me the keys to exercise authority and power to lose and to bind. Holy Spirit, I rely on Your leading.

107. Prayer for discernment:

Daniel 2:28 (NASB): "However, there is a God in heaven who reveals secrets, and He has made known to King Nebuchadnezzar what will take place in the latter days. This was your dream and the visions in your mind *while* on your bed."

*Pray after me:* Jehovah, the Revealer of mysteries, make me see what You are revealing at this time; let scales of blindness fall off my eyes. I return glory to You for hearing my request.

108. Prayer to humble the proud via word of knowledge and discernment:

Daniel 2:47 (BSB): "The king said to Daniel, 'Your God is truly the God of gods and Lord of kings, the Revealer of Mysteries, since you were able to reveal this mystery.'"

*Pray with me:* Father, in the name of Jesus, may You humble kings and princes through your wondrous works in and through my life. You who know the deep secrets of men and reveal mysteries to your servants, may You confound the wise and humble the proud.

109. Prayers to activate and engage the resurrection grace and power (109-114):

John 11:43–44 (NKJV): "Now when He had said these things, He cried with a loud voice, 'Lazarus, come forth!' And he who had died came out bound hand and foot with graveclothes, and his face was wrapped with a cloth. Jesus said to them, 'Loose him, and let him go.'"

*Pray after this manner:* Lord Jesus, You are resurrection and life; You demonstrated the power to raise the dead, to release that grace unto us to do like manner. At the tomb, the Holy Spirit acted on the body of Christ and raised Him from the dead. I ask for supernatural faith and grace to minister resurrection grace as led by Your Spirit, and when such occasion arises.

110. First Kings 17:21–22 (KJB): "And he stretched himself upon the child three times, and cried unto the LORD, and said, O LORD my God, I pray thee, let this child's soul come into him again. And the LORD heard the voice of Elijah; and the soul of the child came into him again, and he revived."

*Pray after this manner:* In the name of the Father, Son, and Holy Spirit, I call back your soul to return to your body now. I transfer the Spirit of grace and resurrection on your body; arise and live!

111. Luke 7:14–15 (BSB): "Then He went up and touched the coffin, and those carrying it stood still. 'Young man,' He said, 'I tell you, get up!' And the dead man sat up and began to speak! Then Jesus gave him back to his mother."

*Pray like this:* Father, in the name above every name; Jesus Christ of Nazareth, I speak life into ears of the dead; hear me now, arise and live again by the power of the resurrected Christ.

112. Second Kings 4:32–35 (NKJV): "When Elisha came into the house, there was the child, lying dead on his bed. He went in therefore, shut the door behind the two of them, and prayed to the LORD. And he went up and lay on the child, and put his mouth on his mouth, his eyes on his eyes, and his hands on his hands; and he stretched himself out on the child, and the flesh of the child became warm. He returned and walked back and forth in the house, and again went up and stretched himself out on him; then the child sneezed seven times, and the child opened his eyes."

*Pray in this manner:* Oh Lord, God Almighty, You are a Life-giver; as I lay my hands on this dead body, I transfer the heat of life by the Spirit of God into this body, and I declare in the name of the Lord let the breath of life enter this body now in Jesus' name.

113. Acts 9:40 (NKJV): "But Peter put them all out, and knelt down and prayed. And turning to the body he said, 'Tabitha, arise.' And she opened her eyes, and when she saw Peter she sat up."

*Pray with me:* I lift up my hands and my voice towards heaven as I call on the God of the living, let the power of resurrection activate this dead body and return life into it now in Jesus' name.

114. Acts 20:9–10 (KJB): "And there sat in a window a certain young man named Eutychus, being fallen into a deep sleep: and as Paul was long preaching, he sunk down with sleep, and fell down from the third loft, and was taken up dead. And Paul went down, and fell on him, and embracing him said, Trouble not yourselves; for his life is in him."

*Pray in a like manner:* I believe in the grace of our Lord Jesus Christ that is now resident in me and unto Him, that is able to do exceedingly, abundantly, above all, we can ask or imagine, according to the dynamic power of God at work in me, let this dead body come back to life now!!!

*(NB: The grace and power of resurrection work with the power of supernatural gift of faith. As you pray, believe, and release your faith in God to be used by Him for a miracle of resurrection. Take time to seek God today, and as long as you are led to do so, the God of all grace shall endow you with grace.)*

115. Prayer for desire to be used by God:

Second Timothy 2:20–21 (NKJV): "But in a great house there are not only vessels of *gold* and *silver*, but also of *wood* and *clay*, some for *honor* and some for *dishonor*. Therefore if anyone cleanses himself from the latter, *he will be a vessel for honor, sanctified and useful for the Master, prepared for every good work.*"

*Pray after me:* My Father, my Creator, I am like clay in Your hand, and You are my potter; I pray and ask that You break me, melt me, cleanse me and then mold me into a vessel of honor useful for kingdom mandate and every good work I was created for.

116. Prayer of recommitment to being God's workman:

Ephesians 2:10 (BSB): "For we are God's workmanship, created in Christ Jesus to do good works, which God prepared in advance as our way of life."

*Repeat after me:* In the name of Jesus, today, I make a commitment to serve the Lord. I was prepared to be a sanctuary, purified, and set apart for the Master's use, and that is the way it is. I will stay on course and not be distracted till my Master calls me home.

117. Prayer against the works of the wicked:

Ecclesiastes 10:8 (NKJV): "He who digs a pit will fall into it, and whoever breaks through a wall will be bitten by a serpent."

*Pray after me:* Father God, as I make this prayer, let the pit dug by enemies swallow them up, and those who look for my trouble meet with trouble. Clap your hands, stamp your feet and pray out loud.

118. Prayer that backfires the plot of the wicked:

Proverbs 26:27 (NKJV): "Whoever digs a pit will fall into it, and he who rolls a stone will have it roll back on him."

*Pray with me:* Lord Jesus, my rock, I pray, whoever is setting a trap for me shall be caught by same, let those who get busy digging a pit for me, be buried by same and those who throw a rock against me, be met by the invincible rock, crushing them to nothing. In the mighty name of Jesus.

119. Prayer that turns a hunter into a hunted:

Esther 7:10 (KJB): "So they hanged Haman on the gallows that he had prepared for Mordecai. Then was the king's wrath pacified."

*Pray with me:* My Father, my Fighter, let those trying to commit evil against me be met by evil. Those who set up a poll to hang me shall end up being hanged by the poll. Let the work of the wicked turn against them 100 percent. Clap your hands and pray.

120. Prayer that will set up the enemy after your life for its destruction:

Psalm 7:15 (NKJV): "He made a pit and dug it out, and has fallen into the ditch *which* he made."

*Pray with me:* Great and mighty God, as I clap my hands, stamp my feet, and pray in the name of the Lord, God of heaven and earth, the pit digger is turning around and falling into the pit He dug for my loved ones or me. In Jesus' name.

121. Prayer for celebration of victory:

Psalm 47:1 (KJB): "O clap your hands, all ye people; shout unto God with the voice of triumph."

*Pray after this manner:* As a prophetic act, lift up your hands to heaven and with a loud voice, shout as a victor triumphing, majestically, as you walk around; in Jesus' name, the devil is defeated again.

122. Prayer for releasing a sound of victory:

Psalm 98:4 (KJB): "Make a joyful noise unto the LORD, all the earth: make a loud noise, and rejoice, and sing praise."

*Pray like this:* Father, in the name of Jesus, from the bottom of my heart, I release a shout of Hallelujah, a shout of praise, and a noise that terrifies the camp of the wicked. As I shout seven times, let any spiritual wall of limitation collapse now in Jesus' name.

123. Prayer to activate and demonstrate the power of God:

Second Kings 2:14 (NKJV): "Then he took the mantle of Elijah that had fallen from him, and struck the water, and said, 'Where *is* the

LORD God of Elijah?' And when he also had struck the water, it was divided this way and that; and Elisha crossed over."

*Pray after this manner:* As I submit under the authority and lordship of Jesus, standing in the presence of the God of heaven and earth, I make a declaration over any barrier before me this day, to divide asunder; oh God, make way where there seems to be no way, now as I tap into infinite grace.

124. Prayer to release creative faith through the Word:

Hebrews 4:12 (NASB): "For the word of God is living and active, and sharper than any two-edged sword, even penetrating as far as the division of soul and spirit, of both joints and marrow, and able to judge the thoughts and intentions of the heart."

*Pray after this manner:* Let the grace of God work through me; as I read the Word, I will be it and apply it appropriately. Your Word has spiritual substance that produces creative manifestations. Just as Your Word was made flesh, so it can be made into whatever You desire. By Your permission, I use Your Word as a raw material for creative miracles. When I speak it, let it work through any medium it contacts.

125. Warfare prayer against demonic entities:

First Samuel 17:51 (NKJV): "Therefore David ran and stood over the Philistine, took his sword and drew it out of its sheath and killed him, and cut off his head with it. And when the Philistines saw that their champion was dead, they fled."

*Say with me:* I use the *Word* as a spiritual sword against any giant or demonic entity that dares challenge God's chosen people or me; as I pray in the name of Jesus, let their heads be chopped off, and those against us now begin to flee at the defeat of their leader. Amen.

126. Prayer that uses the Word as a weapon:

Isaiah 49:2 (BSB): "He made My mouth like a sharp sword; He hid Me in the shadow of His hand. He made Me like a polished arrow; He hid Me in His quiver."

*Pray with me:* Father, in the name of Jesus, as I take up a protest against the devil, I ask that Your cross stays behind me, Your Word before me, and that You hide me in Your presence. May Your Word be like a sharp sword through my mouth to demolish all demonic activities set before me.

127. Prayer that uses the Word as a weapon for mass destruction:

Jeremiah 23:29 (NASB): "'Is My word not like fire?' declares the LORD, 'and like a hammer *which* shatters a rock?'"

*Pray with me:* Father, You are the unquenchable fire, the consuming fire, and the protective pillar of fire; Your Word is weightier than anything and can crush whatever is not of the Lord's. Use me to proclaim Your Word wisely, with revelation and great impact.

128. Prayer for preservation and favor for winning battles:

Hebrews 11:34 (BSB): "Quenched the raging fire, and escaped the edge of the sword; who gained strength from weakness, became mighty in battle, and put foreign armies to flight."

*Pray after me:* In the name of Jesus Christ, the Son of the Living God, I escape every plot to consume my life either by strange fire or by the evil sword. I receive the Spirit of might to challenge big battles, and by Your grace, my enemies begin to flee from me.

129. Prayer to apprehend the weapons of the defeated foes:

First Samuel 21:9 (BSB): "The priest replied, 'The sword of Goliath the Philistine, whom you killed in the Valley of Elah, is here; it is wrapped in a cloth behind the ephod. If you want, you may take it. For there is no other but this one.' And David said, 'There is none like it; give it to me.'"

*Pray with me:* I confiscate the weapons of my adversary; I cease their operational devices and their monitoring gadgets, and I take control over all their weaponry, for the Lord has disarmed principalities and powers and has given me victory forevermore.

130. Prayer that breaks demonic stronghold to undelivered answers and results:

Daniel 10:13 (NKJV): "But the prince of the kingdom of Persia withstood me twenty-one days; and behold, Michael, one of the chief princes, came to help me, for I had been left alone there with the kings of Persia."

*Pray after me:* Oh God of heavens army, do not allow me to battle alone, but as I pray today, I ask that You deploy backup angelic assistance from Michael's jurisdiction to help me overpower diabolic resisting forces over my prayers and breakthroughs, in the name of Jesus.

131. Prayer that cancels satanic weapons over our lives:

Isaiah 54:17 (NKJV): "'No weapon formed against you shall prosper, and every tongue *which* rises against you in judgment you shall condemn. This *is* the heritage of the servants of the LORD, and their righteousness *is* from Me,' says the LORD."

*Pray with me:* In the name of Jesus, any satanic weapon fired against me is hereby revoked. Let the arrow be retrieved and refired against the agent of darkness assigned after me. By the authority given to me, I condemn any tongue, any spell, enchantment, evil omen uttered against me. By heavens verdict, they are all nullified.

132. Prayer that agrees with the Lord's decree:

Lamentations 3:37 (KJB): "Who *is* he *that* saith, and it cometh to pass, *when* the Lord commandeth *it* not?"

*Pray after this manner:* My Father, my Commander, the Bible says that the word of a king is powerful. King Jesus, no one can challenge Your spoken word. Your word concerning me is sure, yes and amen; what You say is final. Therefore, I will not settle for any voice contrary to Your word for me. Amen.

133. Prayer for receiving justification by grace:

Romans 3:24 (KJB): "Being justified freely by his grace through the redemption that is in Christ Jesus."

*Pray with me:* Father, thank you for justifying me freely by Your grace; thank you for a divine reversal from death in sin to life in Christ. And thank you for the complete work of redemption for mankind.

134. Prayer that acknowledges the gift of salvation:

Ephesians 2:8 (NASB): "For by grace you have been saved through faith; and this *is* not of yourselves, *it is* **the gift of God**."

*Pray in this manner:* By the grace of God, I have been atoned by the shed blood of Jesus, now redeemed and finally saved. Nothing much did I do to merit the grace and love of God freely given to me. Jesus, I love you and thank you for my gift of salvation free of any charges; I cannot pay for it, not even by works.

135. Prayer that acknowledges the gift of God:

Romans 6:23 (NASB): "For the wages of sin is death, but the gracious gift of God is eternal life in Christ Jesus our Lord."

*Pray after me:* Dear Lord Jesus, thank you for being the gracious gift of God that has saved me from sin and death to eternal life. I know outside Christ there is no life, but in Christ, there is abundance of life.

136. Prayer of gratitude to God for the church:

Philippians 4:6 (AMP): "Do not be anxious *or* worried about anything, but in everything [every circumstance and situation] by prayer and petition with thanksgiving, continue to make your [specific] requests known to God."

*Pray after this pattern:* Father, thank you for last week's service, thank you for Your evidential presence in Your church; I pray for this Sunday's service that You manifest Your presence and power to heal, deliver and set free the captives, we will always return all glory to Your name.

137. Prayer to call on God to attend to petitions:

First Kings 8:28 (NKJV): "Yet regard the prayer of Your servant and his supplication, O LORD my God, and listen to the cry and the prayer which Your servant is praying before You today."

*Pray like this:* My Father in heaven, Your Word says where two or three are gathered in Your name, there in their midst You are present, may You attend to the petitions that are made in this gathering, in Jesus' mighty name.

138. Prayer to the God who hears us:

Isaiah 65:24 (NASB): "It will also come to pass that before they call, I will answer; while they are still speaking, I will listen."

*Pray with me:* Prayer answering God. You never fail nor disappoint anyone. We are gathered in Your presence to call upon

You in prayer. May You listen to our cry and answer our prayers today. For Your Word is yes and amen. We appreciate You for always being there for us.

139. Prayer of repentance and deliverance from carnality:

First John 2:16 (NASB): "For all that is in the world, the lust of the flesh and the lust of the eyes and the boastful pride of life, is not from the Father, but is from the world."

*Pray like this:* Father God, I repent from all forms of lust; I pray and ask that You deliver me from carnal behaviors and thinking. Let the cross destroy the influence of lust of the eyes, the lust of the flesh, and the pride of life that tries to affect my relationship with God. In my weakness, may I find strength and deliverance from You, Lord. In Jesus' name.

140. Prayer for soul-winning:

Proverbs 11:30 (NKJV): "The fruit of the righteous *is a* tree of life, *and he who wins souls is* **wise**."

*Pray with me:* Father, in the name of Jesus, I employ Your divine wisdom and strategies for effective soul-winning. May the grace of God working in and through me be expressed outwardly as a fruitful tree of righteousness prepared for soul-winning and kingdom expansion.

141. Prayer for nations' inheritance and reassurance as God's heritage:

Psalm 33:12 (NASB): "Blessed is the nation whose God is the LORD, the people He has chosen for His own inheritance."

*Pray with me:* As a chosen people and nation, we declare our total allegiance to God Almighty, who has called us from the kingdom of darkness into His marvelous light.

142. Prayer for healing and restoring nations:

Exodus 34:9 (BSB): "'O Lord,' he said, 'if I have indeed found favor in Your sight, my Lord, please go with us. Although this is a stiff-necked people, forgive our iniquity and sin, and take us as Your inheritance.'"

*Pray with me:* Mighty God, Your presence refreshes us; we pray that You do not depart from us; we are humans and full of shortcomings. May You forgive us and restore our inheritance in You. This we ask in the name of Jesus.

143. Prayer for God's favor and restoration to our nations:

Second Chronicles 7:14–15 (KJB): "If my people, which are called by my name, shall humble themselves, and pray, and seek my face, and turn from their wicked ways; then will I hear from heaven, and will forgive their sin, and will heal their land. Now mine eyes shall be open, and mine ears attent unto the prayer that is made in this place."

*Pray after this manner:* This day, we come before You in repentance of our sins as individuals and as a nation; Father, forgive us our trespasses; heal and fully restore us again. Thank you, Lord, for answering us today; we also pray that Your eyes and ears shall focus on the requests and prayers made in the midst of Your people.

144. Prayer of thanksgiving for our daily benefits:

Psalm 68:19 (NKJV): "Blessed *be* the Lord, *Who* daily loads us *with benefits*, the God of our salvation! *Selah*."

*Pray with me:* Thank you, Lord, for supplying our daily needs, and because of Your riches, in glory, we will live to lack nothing. Deliver us from all forms of lack by Your saving grace.

145. Prayer for the gift of a new day:

Psalm 118:24 (NKJV): "This *is* the day the LORD has made; we will rejoice and be glad in it."

*Pray with me:* We appreciate You, Lord, for this day, which You have made and freely given us, that we will be glad and praise You for Your wonderful works. We are indeed grateful to You, Lord.

146. Prayer of gratitude for new souls added to the church:

Acts 2:47 (NKJV): "Praising God and having favor with all the people. And the Lord added to the church daily those who were being saved."

*Pray after me:* By your infinite mercies, we ask that the church be flooded with souls, we receive favor from God for the people that we can reach within and outside our community, and may the message of the Gospel bring conviction and salvation to many.

147. Prayer of gratitude for a speedy increase to the church:

Acts 6:7 (BSB): "So the word of God continued to spread. The number of disciples in Jerusalem grew rapidly, and a great number of priests became obedient to the faith."

*Pray with faith*: Say, Lord, may Your Word grow mightily in this city and beyond. Let there be rapid results in the multiplication of disciples and that many will be obedient to the leading of the Spirit of God to establish their faith in Christ.

148. Prayer that activates our God-given authority:

Luke 10:19 (NKJV): "Behold, I give you the authority to trample on serpents and scorpions, and over all the power of the enemy, and nothing shall by any means hurt you."

*Pray with me:* Today, by faith, I accept and receive the authority given to me over demons and their cohorts. I take up the divine immunity given to me by God over every fiery dart and the evil of Satan.

149. Prayer for mass evangelism and soul-winning:

Acts 11:21 (KJB): "And the hand of the Lord was with them: and a great number believed, and turned unto the Lord."

*Pray with me:* Almighty God, we continue to preach the Gospel and speak of Your goodness; we ask for Your hand to rest upon Your people, the church, sons, and daughters preaching the Gospel and cause a great number of souls to believe and turn to the Lord, Jesus Christ.

150. Prayer against attack on the church:

Acts 12:1 (KJB): "Now about that time Herod the king stretched forth his hands to vex certain of the church."

*Repeat after me:* My father, my Father, as we begin to pray, anyone who attempts to harass the church, God's people, or the body of Christ with their evil sword or agenda, let such be interrupted and intercepted by the mighty, invincible *sword* of Jehovah.

151. Earnest unceasing prayer for the imprisoned brethren:

Acts 12:5 (NKJV): "Peter was therefore kept in prison, but constant prayer was offered to God for him by the church."

*Repeat after me:* Oh God of heavens army, we lift up our voices in prayer as a church; we make demands on the authority of the Word, the name of Jesus, and the government of God. Let any of our brethren imprisoned physically, spiritually, emotionally, and otherwise be released now. Let chains break and fall off, and the prison doors open now in the name of Jesus.

152. Prayer that releases the grace and power of the spoken Word:

Acts 11:15 (NASB): "And as I began to speak, the Holy Spirit fell upon them just as *He did* upon us at the beginning."

a) *Pray after this manner:* Holy Spirit, I am just a vessel which You can fill and work through, I am a temple where You can dwell, I have no power of my own, my prayer is that the will of God be done always, therefore, as I teach/preach the Word, speak and move through my voice and release the grace of God on the people hungry for You.

b) *Pray for the servant of God after this manner:* Dear Lord Jesus, I pray for God's servant that You anoint his voice, as he teaches and preaches, let your Holy Spirit instantly be moving in people's lives to heal, deliver, transform, and empower them during service, public gathering, and anywhere he goes.

153. Pray against every wicked verdict from the kingdom of darkness:

Acts 12:18–19 (NIV): "In the morning, there was no small commotion among the soldiers as to what had become of Peter. After Herod had a thorough search made for him and did not find him, he cross-examined the guards and ordered that they be executed. Then Herod went from Judea to Caesarea and stayed there."

*Pray after me:* Lord, save me early before the dawn of an evil day and cause those assigned to keep me hostage to be in total confusion and commotion. Let them be as a scapegoat and die my death.

154. Prayer for an unstoppable spread of the Word of God:

Acts 12:24 (KJB): "But the word of God grew and multiplied."

Acts 19:20 (KJB): "So mightily grew the word of God and prevailed."

*Repeat after me:* As a church built on rock, the revelation of the Word, we pray that the Word would grow, increase and multiply mightily throughout all regions where it is preached and beyond. Let the earth be filled with the knowledge of the glory of the Lord.

155. Prayer for church growth and spread of the Gospel message:

Mark 2:2 (NIV): "They gathered in such large numbers that there was no room left, not even outside the door, and he preached the word to them."

*Pray with me:* Let the preaching of Your Word produce a pulling, magnetic effect on people for salvation and addition to Your kingdom and church.

156. Prayer for healing from all manner of blood diseases:

Mark 5:27 (NKJV): "When she heard about Jesus, she came behind *Him* in the crowd and touched His garment."

Mark 5:29 (NKJV): "Immediately the fountain of her blood was dried up, and she felt in *her* body that she was healed of the affliction."

*Pray in this manner:* I believe in the declaration of Jesus on the cross; that "*it is finished*;" therefore, I release my faith to receive healing in my body and soul. My mind is healed, my spirit is encouraged, and my emotions are restored. Now I have the peace of God.

157. Prayer for mass evangelism:

Acts 13:44 (NKJV): "On the next Sabbath almost the whole city came together to hear the word of God."

*Pray after me:* We pray that the power of the Holy Spirit would create a hunger for the Word and a pulling effect so that the people of our city will start to gather in great number to hear the Word of God being preached in our services.

158. Prayer for God to use us to publish the Gospel:

Acts 13:49 (KJB): "And the word of the Lord was published throughout all the region."

*Pray in this manner:* In the name of Yeshua Hamashiac, we pray that the Word of the Lord be published all over our city as the waters cover the sea, and from now on, may the Spirit of God begin to move mightily in our cities and the entire nation.

159. Prayer that releases results:

James 4:3 (NKJV): "You ask and do not receive, because you ask amiss, that you may spend *it* on your pleasures."

*Pray after me:* Oh God of heaven and the earth, deliver me from wrong thinking hindering my prayer from being answered, visit my heart, and cause it to incline towards Your ways. In my prayers, let Your will be done.

160. Prayer to unblock every demonic barrier hindering the kingdom's advancement:

First Thessalonians 2:18 (AMP): "For we wanted to come to you—I, Paul, again and again [wanted to come], but Satan hindered us."

*Pray with me:* In the name of Jesus, we override every satanic agenda programmed to hinder God's servants or the church from fully carrying out the kingdom assignments. May the grace of God be multiplied on His people to fulfill His mandate here on earth.

161. Prayer for God to send skillful people to the church:

Exodus 35:35 (NASB): "He has filled them with skill to perform every work of an engraver, of a designer, and of an embroiderer, in violet, purple, *and* in scarlet *material,* and in fine linen, and of a weaver, as performers of every work and makers of designs."

*Pray with me:* Oh God, the vision and mission You have placed in our hands needs people You have empowered with all kinds of skills; I pray that You send them to partner in the work You have called us to do, and may Your church not lack anything needed to fulfill purpose, growth, and expansion.

162. Prayer of affirmation of our identity with Christ:

Proverbs 28:1 (NKJV): "The wicked flee when no one pursues, but the righteous are bold as a lion."

*Pray after me:* God has not given me the spirit of fear, but boldness and sound mind; I have in me the DNA of the lion of the tribe of Judah, let my adversaries tremble and run at my presence because I carry the presence of God.

163. Prayer of faith to fully appropriate our God-given identity in Christ:

Acts 17:28 (NKJV): "For in Him we live and move and have our being, as also some of your own poets have said, 'For we are also His offspring.'"

*Declare with me:* I am complete in Christ, I have His inheritance, I am seated with Him in heavenly places. I will manifest the gifts and calling upon my life because, in Him, I live, move, and have my being fully expressed through the love and the grace of God.

164. Prayer for active evangelism:

Acts 18:9–10 (NIV): "One night the Lord spoke to Paul in a vision: 'Do not be afraid; keep on speaking, do not be silent. For I am with you, and no one is going to attack and harm you, because I have many people in this city.'"

*Pray with me:* Father, reveal to us with clarity how You would want us to invade our city with the Gospel. You have given us boldness to speak; may You ignite in our hearts the zeal to preach and wisdom to do it rightly.

165. Prayer to intercept those assigned to persecute the Gospel preachers:

Acts 13:11 (NASB): "'Now, behold, the hand of the Lord is upon you, and you will be blind and not see the sun for a time.' And immediately a mist and a darkness fell upon him, and he went about seeking those who would lead him by the hand."

*Pray after me:* Oh God, who can stand in Your way? We pray Thee, let those who attempt to stop the message of the Gospel be humbled by the finger of God. Blind those who continuously oppose the message of righteousness and hinder others from receiving the Gospel. By Your power, let the Word prevail and convict many, including the oppositions to the Gospel of Christ.

166. Prayer to appropriate grace for manifesting the power of God:

Acts 19:11–12 (AMP): "God was doing extraordinary *and* unusual miracles by the hands of Paul, so that even handkerchiefs *or* face-towels or aprons that had touched his skin were brought to the sick, and their diseases left them and the evil spirits came out [of them]."

*Pray with me:* Dear Lord Jesus, I submit and subject my body totally for service of the kingdom to bring glory to You always; anoint my hands with a special grace for extraordinary and unusual miracles; let me be used for soul-winning and expansion of Your kingdom.

167. Prayer for the Word of God to increase and spread beyond our houses of worship:

Acts 19:20 (KJB): "So mightily grew the word of God and prevailed."

*Pray with me:* We pray in this city that the Word of the Lord shall continuously grow and prevail mightily across all nooks and crannies of this land. Holy Spirit, do it again. Amen.

168. Prayer to administer self-deliverance:

Isaiah 10:27 (KJB): "And it shall come to pass in that day, that his burden shall be taken away from off thy shoulder, and his yoke from off thy neck, and the yoke shall be destroyed because of the anointing."

*Pray after this manner:* (Repeat daily till you feel relieved of the burden.) Father in heaven, as I pray now, let any burden of sin, any yoke of bondage, be it substance abuse, drug addiction, sexual perversion, habitual sin, stealing, robbery, fraud, spirit of lies, eating habit disorder, suicidal thought, depression, phobia, panic attack, self-inflicted habitual injuries, abnormal behaviors and all kinds of habitual bondages are hereby denounced and destroyed by the cross, the blood, the Word and the name of Jesus. I receive the anointing that destroys yokes and lifts burden.

169. Prayer to disable contrary testimonials and crossing out satanic impediments:

Colossians 2:14 (KJB): "Blotting out the handwriting of ordinances that was against us, which was contrary to us, and took it out of the way, nailing it to his cross."

*Pray with faith:* By the legal blood of Jesus, all forms of ordinances and satanic allegations are hereby blotted out. Satan, you no longer have any claims over me. Your plots have been crossed out on the cross and by the blood of Jesus. I take victory over you now.

170. Prayer that announces our victory over the satanic kingdom:

Colossians 2:15 (NKJV): "Having disarmed principalities and powers, He made a public spectacle of them, triumphing over them in it."

*Pray with me:* Hallelujah, Jesus has conquered Satan. We key into the victory on the finished work of the cross. We are complete in Christ, who is the head of all principality and power, and therefore, all other principalities and powers have been disarmed. Amen.

171. Your daily prayer: (Repeat the Lord's daily prayer intentionally.)

Matthew 6:9–13 (NKJV): "In this manner, therefore, pray: Our Father in heaven, hallowed be Your name. Your kingdom come. Your will be done on earth as *it is* in heaven. Give us this day our daily bread. And forgive us our debts, as we forgive our debtors. And do not lead us into temptation, but deliver us from the evil one. For Yours is the kingdom and the power and the glory forever. Amen."

*Repeat this prayer:* Father in heaven, I honor Your holy name. Supply my daily bread that I may lack nothing. Forgive all my sins, just as I forgive anyone who offends me. Guide my steps so that I do not fall into temptations and evil. Let Your kingdom, dominion, and glory be from everlasting to everlasting.

172. Prayer to receive grace over the sin of unforgiveness:

Matthew 6:14–15 (NKJV): "For if you forgive men their trespasses, your heavenly Father will also forgive you. But if you do not forgive men their trespasses, neither will your Father forgive your trespasses."

*Repeat this prayer:* Dear Lord Jesus, I willfully forgive all those who offended me this day, and I ask that You also forgive me as I may have offended others. Thank you, Father; I am free from all my trespasses.

173. Prayer that attracts angelic assistance:

Psalm 34:7 (NKJV): "The angel of the LORD encamps all around those who fear Him, and delivers them."

*Pray with me:* Father, God, I pray that You command Your angels as written in Your Word to take charge over me. I ask in the name of Jesus that Your angels will deliver me from the evil plots of the enemy.

174. Prayer for protection:

Job 1:10 (BSB): "Have You not placed a hedge on every side around him and his household and all that he owns? You have blessed the work of his hands, and his possessions have increased in the land."

*Pray out loud:* Father, in the name of Jesus, build a hedge of fire around me and my household. Protect my blessing from all evil cankerworms and caterpillars.

175. Prayer of appreciation and gratitude to God:

Psalm 68:19 (NKJV): "Blessed *be* the Lord, *Who* daily loads us *with benefits,* the God of our salvation! *Selah.*"

*Pray with me:* My Lord and my God, I bless You because You are the one who bears our burden day by day, and You are the God of my salvation. I will forever worship You and be grateful for all You do for me daily.

176. Prayer for grace that brings multiplicity:

Job 8:7 (NKJV): "Though your beginning was small, yet your latter end would increase abundantly."

*Pray with me:* The Bible says, "Better is the end of a thing than its beginning." I pray from the grace to finish well in ministry and all heavenly assignments God has trusted in my hands. I tap into the grace for multiplication, enlargements, and great increase that brings glory to the Father.

177. Prayer to kick start your day:

Proverbs 4:18 (KJB): "But the path of the just is as the shining light, that shineth more and more unto the perfect day."

*Pray after me:* Father, your Word says I have been justified through the shed blood of your Son, Jesus. May the light of Your revelation flood my path as I start my daily activities. In the name of Jesus, I am walking in the light of God.

178. Prayer for direction and soul-winning:

Isaiah 52:7 (NIV): "How beautiful on the mountains are the feet of those who bring good news, who proclaim peace, who bring good tidings, who proclaim salvation, who say to Zion, 'Your God reigns!'"

*Pray after this manner:* In the name of Jesus, Holy Spirit, lead me, drive me, carry me to the place where I can win a soul for the kingdom of God. Order my steps to the people You have prepared to receive the Gospel.

179. Prayer for laborers in God's vineyard:

Matthew 9:38 (NIV): "Ask the Lord of the harvest, therefore, to send out workers into his harvest field."

*Pray with me:* Father, we pray Thee to send workmen, laborers, and sincere workers into the harvest field for soul-winning.

180. Prayer that subdues every other power and every other name:

Romans 14:11 (NKJV): "For it is written: '*As* I live, says the LORD, every knee shall bow to Me, and every tongue shall confess to God.'"

Philippians 2:9–11 (NKJV): "Therefore God also has highly exalted Him and given Him the name, which is above every name, that at the name of Jesus every knee should bow, of those in heaven, and of those on earth, and of those under the earth, and *that* every tongue should confess that Jesus Christ *is* Lord, to the glory of God the Father."

*Pray with me:* In the name of Jesus, the Son of the Living God—the most powerful covenanted name with the highest and unlimited dominion. I stand on the authority of Scriptures—the Word of God; I declare that *Jesus* is Lord over every situation; at the mention of that name, everything with a name must bow to the lordship of Jesus.

181. Prayer that calls for light:

Job 11:17 (NKJV): "And *your* life would be brighter than noonday. *Though* you were dark, you would be like the morning."

*Pray with me:* By the grace of God, my life shall shine like a star, brighter and brighter even more than the noonday. May the entrance of the Word shine light more and more in my life till I shall begin to radiate the life and the light of Christ in and through me.

182. Prayer for God's leading to soul-winning:

Romans 10:15 (NIV): "And how can anyone preach unless they are sent? As it is written: 'How beautiful are the feet of those who bring good news!'"

*Pray in this manner:* Lord Jesus, make me a carrier of the good news of the kingdom. I depend on You for direction. Teach me the technics and give me wisdom on catching men for Christ.

183. Prayer to subdue thought patterns contrary to God's will:

Second Corinthians 10:5 (NKJV): "Casting down arguments and every high thing that exalts itself against the knowledge of God, bringing every thought into captivity to the obedience of Christ."

*Pray with me:* In Jesus' name, I cast down every thought, imagination, and agenda that is sourced in my own carnal nature. I only submit myself to hearing from the Holy Spirit. Now by Your grace, I align my thought with Your thought, and whatever is contrary to Your will is rejected and subdued. Amen.

184. Prayer to align with God's will in all we do:

Philippians 2:13 (NKJV): "For it is God who works in you both to will and to do for *His* good pleasure."

*Pray after me:* In the name of Jesus, I pray that the inherent dynamic power of God and His abounding grace release upon me the unction that will propel me to function in line with the will of God for His good pleasure. May I not please man, but in total obedience, let me do what pleases God.

185. Prayer to thank God for the gift of faith and salvation:

Ephesians 2:8 (KJB): "For by grace are ye saved through faith; and that not of yourselves: *it is* the gift of God."

*Pray after me:* Lord God, I thank you for my salvation in Christ and the gift of faith to remain faithful in my new life. I do not rely on my strength, but I lean on You now and forever.

186. Prayer for the grace of God and the opportunity to do greater works in the kingdom:

John 14:12 (NASB): "Truly, truly I say to you, the one who believes in Me, the works that I do, he will do also; and greater *works* than these he will do; because I am going to the Father."

*Pray after me:* My father in heaven, I stand on the authority of Your Word, I believe in Your Son, Jesus, I believe in the works You did through His life. Today I pray that high grace and favor may come upon me for greater works in the kingdom here on earth.

187. Prayer asking God for endowment with special abilities and skills:

Exodus 31:3 (NLT): "I have filled him with the Spirit of God, giving him great wisdom, ability, and expertise in all kinds of crafts."

Exodus 35:35 (NLT): "The LORD has given them special skills as engravers, designers, embroiderers in blue, purple, and scarlet thread on fine linen cloth, and weavers. They excel as craftsmen and as designers."

*Pray like this:* Dear God of heaven and the earth, the Father of our Lord Jesus Christ and the Giver of every good gift. Your Word says that if I ask, it shall be given. I pray today for special skills, talents, wisdom, and supernatural abilities to do extraordinary things for the kingdom of God here on earth.

188. Prayer to remove hindrances:

First Thessalonians 2:18 (NKJV): "Therefore we wanted to come to you—even I, Paul, time and again—but Satan hindered us."

*Pray with me:* I pray in Jesus' name that nothing shall hinder helpers of the Gospel, nor shall anyone hinder my helpers from reaching me.

189. Prayer against satanic attacks over the church:

Matthew 16:18 (NASB): "And I also say to you that you are Peter, and upon this rock I will build My church; and the gates of Hades will not overpower it."

*Pray:* Father, in the name of the Lord, I neutralize every satanic agenda designed to target and destroy Your work in our church, the church of our Lord, Jesus Christ. No gates of hell or hades or death shall prevail against our ministry and the church in Jesus' name.

190. Prayer of vindication from closed doors:

Revelation 5:5 (NKJV): "But one of the elders said to me, 'Do not weep. Behold, the Lion of the tribe of Judah, the Root of David, has prevailed to open the scroll and to loose its seven seals.'"

*Pray with me:* Father God, may You prevail over my situations, open doors for me, and vindicate me from any bondage. I take my deliverance today. Thank you, Jesus, for I am free.

191. Prayer for deliverance, preservation, and protection from all sorts of death traps:

Daniel 6:22 (NASB): "My God sent His angel and shut the lions' mouths, and they have not harmed me, since I was found innocent before Him; and also toward you, O king, I have committed no crime."

*Pray after me:* In the name of Jesus of Nazareth, let the mouth of every evil devouring lion sent from the kingdom of darkness after me be shut supernaturally. I shall see no harm, for I am under angelic watch.

192. Prayer that activates warrior angels on our behalf:

Second Chronicles 32:21 (NASB): "And the LORD sent an angel who destroyed every warrior, commander, and officer in the camp of the king of Assyria. So he returned in shame to his own land. And when he had entered the temple of his god, some of his own sons killed him there with the sword."

*Pray with me:* Oh God of heaven, let the sword of the wicked and weapons of my adversary supernaturally turn against them in the name of Jesus. Father, dispatch warrior angels to disrupt and scatter the enemy warriors and all their weapons begin to turn against them one after the other.

193. Prayer for favor to find rest in the saving power of the Lord:

Second Chronicles 32:22 (BSB): "So the LORD saved Hezekiah and the people of Jerusalem from the hands of King Sennacherib of Assyria and all the others, and He gave them rest on every side."

*Pray with me:* Oh Lord, Your shadow is a covering and protection over me. May You shield me from the arrows of the wicked. Turn the counsel of the wicked to foolishness.

194. Prayer for empowerment to be God's mouthpiece to proclaim His message:

Second Timothy 4:17 (BSB): "But the Lord stood by me and strengthened me, so that through me the message would be fully proclaimed, and all the Gentiles would hear it. So I was delivered from the mouth of the lion."

*Pray with me:* In the name of Jesus, I will always defend the Gospel by the grace of God working in and through my life. I know it is not by might, nor by power, but by Your Spirit.

195. Prayer for divine rescue and intervention:

Second Timothy 4:18 (NASB): "The Lord will rescue me from every evil deed, and will bring me safely to His heavenly kingdom; to Him *be* the glory forever and ever. Amen."

*Pray like this:* Heavenly Father, Your Word says, "You will never leave me nor forsake me." Thank you for standing by me through all trials and temptation. I continue to pray that You rescue me from all forms of evil plots, setups, and traps till You bring me into Your glorious kingdom in heaven.

196. Prayer for supernatural help and deliverance from the snare of wickedness:

First Samuel 17:37 (NKJV): "Moreover David said, 'The LORD, who delivered me from the paw of the lion and from the paw of the bear, He will deliver me from the hand of this Philistine.' And Saul said to David, 'Go, and the LORD be with you!'"

*Pray with me:* Oh God, my Deliverer; though my enemies are many, yet have You been faithful always to deliver me. You are the same God of the day and the night, the same God of yesterday, today, and forevermore, God of the mountain and God of the valley. The omnipresent and omnipotent God, in Your watch, I am saved. Amen and amen.

197. Prayer for angelic assignment to guard and preserve God's people:

Psalm 34:7 (NKJV): "The angel of the LORD encamps all around those who fear Him, and delivers them."

*Pray like this:* I am most grateful to you, Lord, and faithful are You in keeping with Your promise. May Your angel on guard encamp around me and all those who reverence You, in Jesus' mighty name.

198. Prayer to look up to God in all situations:

Psalm 81:10 (NKJV): "I *am* the LORD your God, Who brought you out of the land of Egypt; open your mouth wide, and I will fill it."

*Pray after me:* God, my source and Deliverer, You neither sleep nor slumber. In the same way, You supplied food to Your people day and night, so they lacked nothing, their clothes were torn, nor their sandals worn out. I trust in Your supernatural abilities to meet all my spiritual and natural needs.

199. Prayer that removes obstacles:

Zechariah 4:7 (NKJV): "'Who *are* you, O great mountain? Before Zerubbabel *you shall become* a plain! And he shall bring forth the capstone with shouts of 'Grace, grace to it!'"

*Pray with me:* In the name of Jesus, the name above every situation, let anything standing before me today that hinders my progress be brought down now by the power in Your name. By

Your grace working through me, let the mountain of poverty and lack, sickness and disease, joblessness, evil occurrences, near success syndrome, non-marriages, depression, rejection, be subdued under the feet and lordship of King Jesus.

200. Prayer for God to make a way:

Isaiah 40:4 (BSB): "Every valley shall be lifted up, and every mountain and hill made low; the uneven ground will become smooth, and the rugged land a plain."

*Pray after me:* God of all possibilities, may You make way for me against all odds, challenges, and impossibilities. Send Your angels to go ahead of me to make all crooked ways straight, fill up the valleys on my path, and level the hills on my path. Oh God, make a way where there is no way.

201. Prayer for favor in this new season: the year of the Lord's favor:

Isaiah 61:7 (NKJV): "Instead of your shame *you shall have* double *honor,* and *instead of* confusion they shall rejoice in their portion. Therefore in their land they shall possess double; everlasting joy shall be theirs."

*Repeat after me:* Oh Lord God, trade my pain for fame, my shame for gain, my disgrace for grace. I receive by double honor and portion in the land of the living, double blessing for my trouble; I trade poverty for prosperity, turn my test into testimony in Jesus' name.

202. Prayer declarations for overcomers:

First John 4:4 (NKJV): "You are of God, little children, and have overcome them, because He who is in you is greater than he who is in the world."

*Pray after me:* In the name of Jesus, I have the Greater One on the inside of me; I walk in victory as an overcomer by virtue of the finished work of the cross. Every day I shall live in this world with a victor mentality; I refuse to be victimized by satanic manipulations.

203. Prayer that expels challenging mountains:

Jeremiah 51:25 (BSB): "Behold, I am against you, O destroying mountain, you who devastate the whole earth, declares the LORD. I will stretch out My hand against you; I will roll you over the cliffs and turn you into a charred mountain."

*Pray with me:* Oh, ye mountain of limitations; devouring and tormenting spiritual mountains, hear ye the Word of the Lord, by the hand of Jehovah, be cast off, be leveled off, and be diminished now as I pray in Jesus' name.

204. Prayer for favor, promotion, and diverse upliftment to children of God:

Daniel 2:48–49 (BSB): "Then the king promoted Daniel and gave him many generous gifts. He made him ruler over the entire province of Babylon and chief administrator over all the wise men of Babylon. And at Daniel's request, the king appointed Shadrach,

Meshach, and Abednego to manage the province of Babylon, while Daniel remained in the king's court."

*Prayer after this manner:* Father, Your Word says, "A man's gift makes room for him and brings him before great men." May love and grace of giving open doors to access great people and VIPs. Use me as a helper and ambassador of love. May it come to pass that my brethren would receive promotion through me, in Jesus' name.

205. Prayer to satisfy my spiritual thirst and hunger for God:

Psalm 42:1–2 (NLT): "As the deer longs for streams of water, so I long for you, O God. I thirst for God, the living God. When can I go and stand before him?"

*Pray after me:* Father, Your Word says that blessed are those who hunger and thirst after righteousness, for they shall be filled. Lord Jesus, I am hungry and thirsty for You. I need Your presence more than ever in my life. Whatever is the hindrance from accessing Your presence, help me know it and help me cut off from it.

206. Prayer for supernatural fire of God in my life and household:

Obadiah 1:18 (BSB): "'Then the house of Jacob will be a blazing fire, and the house of Joseph a burning flame; but the house of Esau will be stubble—Jacob will set it ablaze and consume it. Therefore, no survivor will remain from the house of Esau.' For the LORD has spoken."

*Pray with me:* Holy Spirit, make me a blazing fire and my house a burning flame that will be too dangerous for all sorts of witchcraft activities and demonic manipulations. My house shall be a no-fly zone for the devil and his cohorts. This I pray in Jesus' name.

207. Prayer for the dynamic power and grace of God:

Ephesians 3:20 (NKJV): "Now to Him who is able to do exceedingly abundantly above all that we ask or think, according to the power that works in us."

*Pray after me:* I thank God for His residing grace in me. I know who I am and what I have. The power of God is inside of me; by His grace, I am what God says I am, I will be what God says I will be, and I will do what God says I will do.

208. Prayer to avert (stop) mockery:

Psalm 79:10 (NKJV): "Why should the nations say, 'Where *is* their God?' Let there be known among the nations in our sight the avenging of the blood of Your servants *which has been* shed."

*Pray with me:* Jehovah, our defender, do not let unbelievers make a mockery of us and say, "Where is our God?" God of vengeance, fight for us and grant us a righteous verdict.

209. Prayer to nullify the plot of the enemy:

Acts 12:11 (ESV): "When Peter came to himself, he said, 'Now I am sure that the Lord has sent his angel and rescued me from the hand of Herod and from all that the Jewish people were expecting.'"

*Pray with me:* Oh God, my Helper, come rescue me from the hand of my oppressors, dispatch an angel for my aid, and may the plan and expectation of the wicked come to nothing; in Jesus' name, I pray.

210. Prayer that activates the atmosphere for deliverance:

Obadiah 1:17 (KJB): "But upon mount Zion shall be deliverance, and there shall be holiness; and the house of Jacob shall possess their possessions."

*Pray with me:* Father, in the name of Jesus, let this arena supernaturally turn into a holy mount Zion so that we may experience deliverance from all sorts of demonic strongholds and be free to possess our possessions. I am free from poverty, lack, sickness, and reproach, in Jesus' name.

211. Prayer that motivates the intercessor:

Isaiah 40:31 (NKJV): "But those who wait on the LORD shall renew *their* strength; they shall mount up with wings like eagles, they shall run and not be weary, they shall walk and not faint."

*Pray after me:* Oh God, my Father, may I find and receive strength in You, that I may not get weary and faint in my walk with God. I receive renewed strength every day as I continue to wait on God.

212. Prayer to break the barriers of delay:

Deuteronomy 1:6–8 (NKJV): "The LORD our God spoke to

us in Horeb, saying: 'You have dwelt long enough at this mountain. Turn and take your journey, and go to the mountains of the Amorites, to all the neighboring *places* in the plain, in the mountains and in the lowland, in the South and on the seacoast, to the land of the Canaanites and to Lebanon, as far as the great river, the River Euphrates. See, I have set the land before you; go in and possess the land which the LORD swore to your fathers—to Abraham, Isaac, and Jacob—to give to them and their descendants after them.'"

*Pray with me:* In the name of Jesus, the power of delay is broken. Whatever has caused me to be long overdue on one spot, let that siege be broken off me in the mighty name of Jesus. I decree and declare it is my time to possess all that God has freely given me.

## Back Cover Page

Daily devotion and intercessory prayer lifestyle generate a dynamic, spiritual walk with God that makes the supernatural a natural way of living on this planet earth.

If you need oxygen to breathe and live, then you need prayer to live and walk in the Spirit. Prayer is the power supply center for every living church. Without intercession and prayer warriors, the ministry will experience untold frustrations and defeat from the gates of Hades. Just as the ministry of Jesus was backed with prayer and intercession, so too must the church or any ministry be supported by the pillar of intercession. A ministry with a strong prayer and intercessory team will be powerful, demonstrating the supernatural manifestations of the Holy Spirit in various dimensions.

In this book, you will learn how to use the right phrases and scriptural applications in your daily prayer and devotion. In a short time, you are about to become a spiritual dynamite from the impartation you will receive as you use this book. The Holy Spirit, the Spirit of supplication and grace, the Spirit of intercession, shall teach and help you pray effectively. It is time to engage your faith as you commune with God in prayer and intercession.

## About the Author

Manasseh Omechamba is a US-based Revivalist and founder of The Evangelistic Allied Ministries International, also known as Team International Church, with branches from around the world. His unique calling and anointing have made a clear distinction as a firebrand minister and have shown great impact in the supernatural power and move of the Holy Spirit in the body of Christ. He operates in a strong Apostolic and Prophetic unction with a vision to bring restoration to the church and to engage the supernatural power of God. He is married to Pastor Ernestine and is blessed with three sons. He is the author of the book *The Spirit of Prophecy* and *Prayer Power Point*, among others. He is, at the moment of writing this book, a doctoral student in Christian leadership/administration.

### Contact Information

The Evangelistic Allied Ministries International
(Alias Team International Church)
Head Quarters: Columbus Ohio
Email: supernaturalhouseofprayer@gmail.com
Tel. +16145894767
WhatsApp: +2349016530594
WhatsApp: +16145894767
Website: www.teami.info
Facebook page: Team International Church
Facebook Profile: Shepherd Manasseh Omechamba
YouTube Channel: Shepherd Manasseh Omechamba
Instagram: Shepherd Manasseh Omechamba

CPSIA information can be obtained
at www.ICGtesting.com
Printed in the USA
LVHW012110291122
734192LV00014B/681

9 781685 569112